Contested Boundaries

Contested Boundaries:
New Critical Essays on the Fiction of Toni Morrison

Edited by

Maxine L. Montgomery

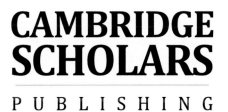

CAMBRIDGE SCHOLARS

PUBLISHING

Contested Boundaries:
New Critical Essays on the Fiction of Toni Morrison,
Edited by Maxine L. Montgomery

This book first published 2013

Cambridge Scholars Publishing

12 Back Chapman Street, Newcastle upon Tyne, NE6 2XX, UK

British Library Cataloguing in Publication Data
A catalogue record for this book is available from the British Library

ISBN (10): 1-4438-5150-7, ISBN (13): 978-1-4438-5150-3

CONTENTS

Acknowledgements vii

Introduction 1
Maxine Lavon Montgomery

Part I: 'Are You Afraid?': Merciful Haunting in a New World Setting

Chapter One... 14
"These Careful Words . . . Will Talk to Themselves": Textual Remains
and Reader Responsibility in Toni   Morrison's *A Mercy*
Maria Rice Bellamy

Part II: 'A Slave By Choice': Re-reading the (Neo) Slave Narrative

Chapter Two 34
The (Neo)Slave Narrative in Black and White: Toni Morrison's
Re-Envisioning of Masculinity in *A Mercy*
Gene Melton, II

Chapter Three 53
Becoming a She-Lion: Sexual Agency in Toni Morrison's *Beloved*
and *A Mercy*
Alice Eaton

Chapter Four.. 67
The Natural and Legal Geographies of the Body: Law's Corpus Written
on the Lives of Sethe and Florens
Kathryn Mudgett

Part III: 'To Be Female in This Place is To Be An Open Wound That Cannot Heal': Memory, Trauma, and Maternal Loss

Chapter Five 82
'To Be One or to Have One': 'Motherlove' in The Fiction of Toni Morrison
Terry Otten

Chapter Six 96
'Mother Hunger': Trauma, Intra-Feminine Identification, and Women's Communities in Toni Morrison's *Beloved*, *Paradise*, and *A Mercy*
Sandra Cox

Part IV: 'It Was Not a Grace; It was A Mercy': Spirituality in the Americas

Chapter Seven.. 126
'More Sinned Against Than Sinning': Redefining Sin and Redemption in *Beloved* and *A Mercy*
Shirley A. Stave

Part V: 'This Land is Our Home . . . But I am Exile Here': Alternative Geographies

Chapter Eight... 144
Post Racialism and its Discontents: The Pre-National Scene in Toni Morrison's *A Mercy*
Charles Tedder

Contributors.. 160

ACKNOWLEDGEMENTS

In any scholarly undertaking, there are those individuals who labor behind the scenes, out of sight, quietly but persistently, in ways that enable a project to come into fruition. I am indebted to a host of people for the role each has played during the course of this editorial venture. First, I would like to thank my students not only for sharing my enthusiasm for Morrison's work, but also their willingness to offer fresh insights about the author's canon and the larger issues she engages. I am fortunate to be able to teach students who are not afraid to rethink established ideas about literature, culture, and the human experience, challenging all of us to envision the world in a nuanced light. I owe a debt as well to Florida State University's Office of Faculty Research for awarding a grant that allowed me time away from teaching so that I could edit much of this volume. I would be remiss if I did not mention my thanks to the scholars whose work appears in this collection. Without you, your brilliant ideas, your keen critical intellect, your willingness to invest in this project, *Contested Boundaries* would not be possible. Last, but certainly not least, I want to thank my family – my husband Nathaniel Crawford and our daughter Samantha Natalya Crawford – for your love, patience, and support. You inspire me to dream and dare.

INTRODUCTION

MAXINE LAVON MONTGOMERY

Although Toni Morrison was comfortably situated among an elite group of writers at the vanguard of belles lettres decades before the publication of *A Mercy*, the fall 2008 release of her ninth novel has occasioned a reappraisal of not only her canon but also her position on the global literary scene. One might attribute this reevaluation to reviews which placed the highly anticipated novel in conversation with her earlier fiction. A recent international conference in Paris was devoted to a reexamination of her writing. The summer 2011 publication of a MELUS special issue dedicated to an investigation of new directions in the criticism surrounding her work prompted further reassessment of the author's evolving oeuvre. Aside from the interest scholars and critics have generated, it is Morrison who provides the initial impetus for a re-reading of her canon in lieu of the publication of her 2008 novel when she describes mercy as the "heartbeat" of her third novel, *Song of Solomon*:

> "Mercy," the other significant term, is the grace note; the earnest though, with one exception, unspoken wish of the narrative's population. Some grant it; some never find it; one, at least, makes it the text and cry of her extemporaneous sermon upon the death of her granddaughter. It touches, turns and returns to Guitar at the end of the book – he who is least deserving of it – and moves him to make it his own final gift. It is what one wishes for Hagar; what is unavailable to and unsought by Macon Dead, senior; what his wife learns to demand from him, and what can never come from the white world as is signified by the inversion of the name of the hospital from Mercy to "no-Mercy." It is only available from within. The center of the narrative is flight; the springboard is mercy. [1]

If mercy is the unspoken wish within or the discursive springboard for *Song of Solomon*, then it resonates broadly as the silent, albeit impassioned collective plea on part of all the fictional characters who people her novelistic universe. Morrison's characters operate within an imaginary geography where grace is ever-present, yet, as Baby Suggs points out in her improvisational sermon, tantalizingly beyond reach. For obvious reasons, critics refer to *A Mercy* as a prequel to Morrison's Pulitzer Prize-winning and decisively most acclaimed novel *Beloved*.[2] Such an assertion is illuminating on one level, but at the same time it encourages a dangerous oversimplification of the author's ambitious, increasingly global narrative project involving an excavation of America's raced past. *A Mercy*, with its spotlight on a worldwide network of fictional characters, represents her efforts at upsetting race in ways that complicate fundamental concerns throughout her canon.[3] This should come as no surprise to Morrison's readers who realize that objective reality is under constant inspection in her fiction. Indeed, much of the enduring appeal of her writing stems from her ability to challenge old ways of knowing, predictable ways of thinking, and established ways of seeing. Scholars therefore must be wary of any approach to Morrison's work that relies upon a reductive analysis of cultural markers, lest we, like the naïve, love-struck Florens, misread the signs marking the path along the author's expanding artistic and political journey.

This volume aims to map the space between *A Mercy,* Morrison's ninth and arguably most enigmatic novel, and the fiction comprising the author's multiple- text canon. *Contested Boundaries* accomplishes this through the inclusion of eight original essays representing a range of critical approaches that trouble narrative boundaries demarcating the novels included in Morrison's evolving opus, with *A Mercy* serving as a locus for discussion of her re-figuration of concerns central to her narrative project. Issues relevant to the conflicted mother-child relationship, the haunting legacy of slavery, the black female body as site of trauma, the thorny quest for an idealized home, the perilous transatlantic journey, and, yes, the desire for mercy recur, but they do so with a difference, a "Morrisonian" twist that demands close intellectual inquiry. Essays included in this volume are invested in a persistent scholarly investigation of this narrative and rhetorical play.

Literary critics have noted the formal pattern of repetition-with-a-difference that obtains in the African-American narrative.[4] An examination of key moments in Morrison's fiction reveals the presence of a discursive lineage traceable to precursor events and texts within and outside the black canonical tradition. In discussing the inspiration for *A Mercy*, Morrison mentions her efforts at fictionalizing events surrounding Bacon's Rebellion.[5] But her re-inscription of the 1679 revolt, much like her reworking of the story of Margaret Garner, reveals a reliance upon numerous, often competing narrative perspectives in ways that represent an effort to not only worry the borderlines between history and fiction, but also expand the lens through which America views the past.

Liminality, in a spatial, metaphysical, and discursive sense, is central to an understanding of Morrison's canon, and more than any other space, the Middle Passage functions a locus for theorizing about the quirky connection linking the novels that comprise her fictional canon. For Morrison as well as countless other black writers, "re-memory," a psychic journey back to the past, offers a stay against the psychological ravages associated with the transatlantic journey; it is in its broadest sense a mnemonic resistance against the rupture owing to the forced migration of blacks from Africa to the New World. Along these lines, the mother figure is a source of unmediated memory – a vital link with a lost past existing outside the perimeter of a patriarchal, capitalist, and Western construct. Hortense Spillers traces the development of black literary and cultural production in underscoring not only the dislocation associated with the Middle Passage but also the primacy of the feminine as the solution to self-identity.[6] Drawing upon psychoanalysis and feminism, Bracha Ettinger uses the term "matrixial borderspace" in describing the presence of an undifferentiated gender space allowing for the creation of a self not tied to fixed notions of masculine or feminine.[7] No longer is the law of the father the primary means of selfhood. Instead, there is a co-existent link between male and female – a radically reconfigured connection that is a site for the development of an altogether new, hybrid persona.

Narrative action in a great deal of Morrison's fiction occurs within a familial context involving the broken mother-daughter bond as she directs attention to the attempt on the part of the female subject to (re)define the self in the absence of a monolithic past or mother tongue. Much of what happens in her fiction takes place in the interstitial place connecting the guilty mother and abandoned child. Language is at the center of this dyad. Through discourse Morrison endeavors to bridge the gulf – in psychological, geographic, and linguistic terms – between estranged female Diaspora personae. The inventive use of dialogue among a community of slaves and ex-slaves reveals the existence of a complex lineage that mediates against simplistic genealogical notions embedded in the American origins narrative, however. In Morrison's fiction, there is no such thing as a singularly constituted past or a heritage that one can easily recover. Beloved, the titular character of the author's Pulitzer Prize-winning novel, speaks in a lyrical voice that is traceable only in part to Sethe's African-born mother Nan. The ghost-child's accent also finds its pre colonial beginnings in Florens' poetic voice – one that is not only 'speakerly,' but 'writerly' as well, suggesting the influence of an African mother and kindly Anglo Saxon priests. Even so, with her trek in search of the nameless blacksmith, Florens is indebted more to the naturalist insights gleaned from an American Indian cultural tradition and "re-memory" than to oral or written discourse, despite her confessional gesture of writing her life's story onto the walls of Jacob Vaark's abandoned home.

II.

Events transpiring on the national and international scene during the decades following the publication of *Beloved* reflect a change in dominant attitudes surrounding the politics of race and nationhood. Not only is this shift mirrored in the public rhetoric of political debate, it is evident in the realm of cultural studies and the literature produced at the turn of the last century. Chief among the events engaging the political and artistic imagination of writers and scholars alike is the emergence of globalism, with issues of cross cultural influence and their relevance to a so-called nationalist identity. Scholars such as Paul Gilroy, Homi Bhabha, Edward Said, Gayatri Spivak, Carol Boyce Davies, and others are positioned at the forefront of intellectual conversation about the implications of migration and transnational exchange for a displaced, progressively more international population. Discussions about the viability of a monolithic Caribbean literary lineage or the need for a remapping of an American 'writerly' tradition along global lines underscore the need to rethink established conceptions of history and canon along with the ideologies surrounding such formulations. Time, space, and identity undergo relentless renegotiation in an era characterized by border crossing of epic proportions. In this regard, ideas of genealogical influence, in both a literary and biological sense, are under intense interrogation as scholars carry out a more nuanced articulation and investigation of geopolitical sites of beginning.

In "Home," Morrison situates the mass migration of a raced population during the modern and contemporary eras within a socio-cultural and historic context involving chattel slavery. "The contemporary world's work," she points out, "has become policing, halting, forming policy regarding, and trying to administer the movement of people. Nationhood – the very definition of citizenship – is constantly being demarcated and re-demarcated in response to exiles, refugees, *Gastarbeiter*, immigrants, migrations, the displaced, the fleeing, and the besieged" (10). She offers a compelling reading of world history in terms of slavery and the transatlantic journey as catalysts for cultural and socio-political production. What begins as a discussion of race and home – the two major priorities in her narrative project – develops into a meditation on the paradigmatic quest for a utopian home free of racial restraint. For

Morrison as well as countless other writers, race, language, and home are mutually dependent constructs; they coexist in ways suggestive of the struggle on the part of the raced author for literary authority and autonomy.

Morrison is not only a prolific creative artist whose decades-long career, literary output, and worldwide acclaim have proven her staying power on an international scene, she is also a public figure often at the center of intellectual debates. It is difficult to disassociate her writing from the socio-political milieu out of which her work evolves. In 1987, a group of forty-eight prominent writers and critics protested when *Beloved* failed to win the National Book Award or National Book Critics Circle Award. They signed a tribute to her career and published it in the 24 January 1988 edition of the *New York Times* Book Review. Morrison was awarded a Pulitzer Prize for *Beloved* in 1988, and in 1993 she became the first African-American woman to win the Nobel Prize. Early in 2011, a group of scholars and creative writers selected *Beloved* as the most significant work of fiction in the last twenty-five years, a fitting, if not ironic recognition in light of the previous rebuff.

Conceptions of the borderlands as disputed terrain surface and resurface in the decades following the publication of *Beloved*. These ideas are manifest in escalating policy debates on immigration in the aftermath of September 11, 2001. They find expression in troubling references to those displaced as a result of Hurricane Katrina as "refugees." Such ideas also enter into twenty-first century scholarly conversations about the recuperation of African-American Literary history. What is prevalent is the idea of geography as contested ground subject to ongoing upheaval, change, and flux. Throughout this time, race continues as a persistent fact at the center of public and private life. The modest gains achieved as a result of the modern Civil Rights Movement along with the elimination of race-based preferences in university admissions and employment decisions prompt discussion of a society where color no longer matters. If there is a singular event that signals this thinking it is the 2008 election of Barack Obama as the country's first black present. Morrison's ninth novel and early critical response to the text raise important questions about race – specifically, the viability of a post racial America. Publishers scheduled the release of *A Mercy* to coincide with Mr. Obama's election. Morrison endorsed him for president and openly supported him during his campaign, lauding him for being a candidate whose wisdom and moral center transcend issues of race, class, or gender ("Letter to Barack Obama," *New York Observer*, January 28, 2008). Although one may argue that Morrison's words lend currency to the discourse surrounding post racial thinking, she is far from sanctioning utopian notions of a society where race no longer matters.

   Beloved, the author's most controversial novel, appeared as the first in a loosely constructed trilogy including *Jazz* and *Paradise*. In the years following the release of the Pulitzer Prize-winning work of fiction Morrison expands her reputation as a creative writer, essayist, cultural critic, playwright, song writer, and editor. On May 29, 2012, President Obama awarded her with the Medal of Freedom, the nation's highest civilian honor. Now in her eighties, she publishes a play, *Desdemona*, and her tenth novel, *Home*, a fictional account of the events surrounding the Korean War. But it is the release of *A Mercy* that constitutes a watershed moment in her lengthy and auspicious career. With her ninth novel, she re-inscribes key moments in the nation's pre-vcolonial history using a uniquely twenty-first century subject position. Morrison engages past events in ways that are old, yet paradoxically new. For her, the era designated as 'post' is itself a borderspace, a disjunctive moment rife with meaning in terms of her narrative and rhetorical choices. Homi Bhabha describes the essence of this positioning: "The borderline work of culture demands an encounter with 'newness' which is not part of the continuum of past and present. It creates a sense of the new as an insurgent act of cultural translation. Such art does not merely recall the past as social cause or aesthetic precedent; it renews the past, refiguring it as a contingent 'in-between' space, that innovates and interrupts the performance of the present" (*The Locations of Culture* 7). Morrison's re-inscription of the ad hoc Early American setting of *A Mercy* allows her to carry out what Bhabha aptly refers to as an "act of cultural translation." Her ninth novel revises the dynamics involved in chattel slavery and the lingering effects on successive generations, even as the institution and its associated social relations are reframed, linked with race neutral, twenty-first century concerns of consumer capitalism, imperialism, and the perils associated with heterosexual love. Not only that, but the Middle Passage, site of rupture and "re-memory," is re-envisioned in ways that point to an erasure of national bounds. Publication of *A Mercy* represents a climactic moment in Morrison's evolving political consciousness, her fictional geography, and, consequently, a shift in the margins marking her multiple-text universe. The complicated markers of difference figuring in "Recitatif" and continuing with *Paradise* and *Love* culminate in the author's ninth work of fiction. This volume ventures to chart that change, not for the sake of encoding it, but in an attempt to open up new ways of interrogating her writing.

III.

Contested Boundaries therefore pursues several lines of scholarly inquiry: first, the volume seeks to examine the ways in which *A Mercy* signals a new direction in the author's developing canon; second, the essays included ask how a sustained reading of the novel might shed fresh light on recurring themes, issues, or subjects familiar to Morrison's readers; finally, this project endeavors to situate Morrison's ninth work of fiction within the larger discursive framework of the author's novelistic universe.

This volume includes essays by established as well as emerging scholars. All essays are original and written specifically for this collection. Three of the eight essays evolve out of papers presented at academic conferences. The scholars whose work appears here have drawn upon a range of critical and theoretical approaches, including feminism, eco feminism, trauma theory, critical race theory, and post colonialism. With each essay, there is an attempt to avoid the use of esoteric language so as to make the volume accessible to a broad scholarly audience.

Contested Boundaries relies upon a five-part organizational scheme that foregrounds concerns recognizable to Morrison's works of fiction. Section titles take their cue from signal moments in *A Mercy* – rupturing moments serving as sites of scholarly meditation on the disjuncture between Morrison's novels. Each essay not only takes up the issue of boundaries – in a narrative, metaphysical, or geographic sense --, it also seizes upon *A Mercy* as fertile textual grounds for a revisionist reading of Morrison's fiction, from *The Bluest Eye* to her most recent novel *Home*.

Part One, 'Are You Afraid?': Merciful Haunting in a New World Setting, includes Maria Rice Bellamy's essay, "These Careful Words . . . Will Talk To Themselves": Textual Remains and Reader Responsibility in Toni Morrison's *A Mercy*, which focuses on how child abandonment creates a "haunting presence" in both *Beloved* and *A Mercy*. Attending to ideas current in recent scholarship on contemporary forms of haunting and counterpointing that understanding with an investigation of *A Mercy's* experiential rhetorical structure involving the use of written and verbal texts, she focuses on the figure of the abandoned child and the haunting presences that remain at the end of the novel. Demonstrating that Morrison's ninth novel engages multiple forms of child abandonment during a period of rapid social change, that the novel's orphaned characters are complexly fashioned, she contends that *A Mercy* "draws Morrison's readers into a different discursive space than many recent literary representations of haunting, including *Beloved*." Through an investigation of the contemporary readers' responsibility and the role of "re-memory," to borrow Morrison's term, Bellamy makes a compelling case for an understanding of the ways in which Morrison's ninth novel "leaves the characters and readers of *A Mercy* in the haunted middle space of survival and witness." Reliance upon memory as a recuperative act enables Morrison to create a dynamic interaction among her novels, and the insight that we gain from this text encourages the reader to revisit the author's other works and view them from an original, more liberatory point of view.

The three essays included in Part Two, 'A Slave By Choice': Re-reading the (Neo) Slave Narrative, situate Morrison's fifth and ninth novels against a literary backdrop of the slave narrative genre. In "The (Neo) Slave Narrative in Black and White: Toni Morrison's Re-Envisioning of Masculinity in *A Mercy*, Gene Melton, II is concerned with the search for manhood on the part of the novel's assortment of male figures – black and white, slave and free, heterosexual and homosexual. Drawing upon the work of James Olney and others, Melton offers a reading of the Blacksmith, Willard, Scully, Jacob Vaark, and D'Ortega in terms of Morrison's experimentation with the boundaries of the slave narratives' portrait of racialized masculinity. Melton rightly concludes that Morrison's ninth novel enlargers the established limits of the neo slave narrative as "an inclusive genre that comprehends the experiences of slaves and former slaves, black and white, 'slave' and 'free.'"

Alice Eaton examines the trajectory of Morrison's fiction in terms of a progression to "a more radical vision of female sexuality." In "Becoming a She-Lion: Sexual Agency in Toni Morrison's *Beloved* and *A Mercy*," Eaton argues that sexual expression for both Beloved and Florens is rooted in slavery and attempts to proscribe female sexuality in ways that privilege a capitalist, patriarchal system. Eaton analyzes sexual expression as an important, positive impulse, although she also acknowledges that the "she-lion" as a figure both signifies empowerment for women and the terrifying specter of a deeply wounded woman.

For Kathryn Mudgett in "The Natural and Legal Geographies of the Body: Law's Corpus Written on the Lives of Sethe and Florens," it is the written and unwritten codes of pre-colonial America that reinforce the social order delimiting the identity and aspirations of the slave and ex-slave communities. Mudgett takes a law and literature approach to Morrison's fifth and ninth novels by showing how the law inscribes the status of the slave as person and property. Mudgett thus examines the idea of home – one of Morrison's most frequent themes – as an aspect of life denied to African-Americans.

Much of the action in Morrison's novels takes place in the interstitial space between the guilty, estranged mother and abandoned child. Essays included in Part Three, "To Be Female in This Place is to Be an Open Wound That Cannot Heal: Memory, Trauma, and Maternal Loss," direct attention to the emotional trauma associated with "motherloss" and the attempt on the part of Morrison's female characters to recreate a sense of wholeness in the face of maternal that loss. Whereas in "'To Be One or Have One': Mother Love in the Fiction of Toni Morrison," Terry Otten examines the ironic, if not destructive potential of love and the ways a perverse, capitalistic slave system "transfigures 'motherlove' into a potential weapon," Sandra Cox discusses maternity as a site of trauma and identification. Relying heavily upon the work of contemporary trauma theorists, Cox's "'Mother-Hunger': Trauma, Intra-feminine Identification, and Women's Communities in Toni Morrison's *Beloved*, *Paradise*, and *A Mercy*" offers a reading of a trio of Morrison's novels as "a complicating reply to the preceding one." Ultimately, Cox astutely points out, *A Mercy* does not prove to be a space where intra-feminine community figures as a therapeutic response to the collective and personal trauma inflicted upon the female community.

Part Four, 'It Was Not a Miracle'; 'It Was a Mercy': Spirituality in the Americas, includes Shirley Stave's "'More Sinned Against Than Sinning': Re-defining Sin and Redemption in *Beloved* and *A Mercy*," which takes an uncompromising approach to Morrison's allusions to Christianity, arguing that Morrison adamantly critiques Christianity through her fifth and ninth novels. Focusing on Morrison's feminist rewriting of Christian theology, Stave observes that even though redemption is possible in *Beloved*, in *A Mercy*, "community is worthless, based upon a biblical patriarchal model."

Part Five, 'This Land is Our Home . . . But . . . I am Exile Here': Alternative Geographies," includes Charles Tedder's "Post Racialism and its Discontents: The Pre National Scene in Toni Morrison's *A Mercy*," which examines Morrison's ninth novel as a recuperation of history through acts of remembrance, revision, and recursion. Tedder grapples with what he refers to as the "national primal scene" that prompts readers to undergo the work of "re-memory" vis-à-vis the colonial period. Drawing on the work of Werner Sollors, Stuart Hall, Karl Popper, and others, he explores the ways that *A Mercy* creates an alternative mytho-utopian past for the national narrative of America, specifically by imagining a multi-ethnic colonial landscape that contradicts the centrality of American Literature's concern with the "new white man" Morrison describes in *Playing in the Dark*. He argues that the symbolic action of Morrison's novels plays upon notions of a post-ethnic identity, and the shared past she remembers insists on an anti-racist American identity that is, in some sense, the truest one – or at least the most complete.

The eight essays collected here point to *A Mercy*, a slim novel that has received mostly positive critical attention, as a meditational pause along the course of Morrison's decades-long literary career. Rather than marking the end of her journey, the publication of her ninth novel occasions an opportunity for author, scholar, and critic alike to glance back and forward simultaneously.[12] This volume underscores the need to construct a literary historiography that accommodates disjuncture and dissonance rather than one clamoring for artificially imposed cohesion. Scholars contributing to this collection reveal a willingness to engage in the kind of intellectual heavy lifting that such an enterprise demands, even as their essays insist upon the need to uncouple Morrison's fiction from often arbitrarily enforced theoretical limits.

Notes

[1] "Unspeakable Things, Unspoken: The Afro-American Presence in American Literature." *Michigan Quarterly Review* 28.1 (1989): 29.

[2] See, for example, Hilary Mantel, "How Sorrow Became Complete." *The Guardian*. November 8, 2008. Mantel asserts that "Morrison is evoking the spirit of *Beloved* rather than creating something new." Maggie Galehouse offers a similar reading of the two novels in her review in *The Houston Chronicle*, November 9, 2008. Finally, Michiko Kakutani reads *A Mercy* as "a kind of prelude to *Beloved.*" *The New York Times*, November 3, 2008. Jessica Wells Cantiello presents a thorough assessment of early reviews of Morrison's latest novel in "From Pre-Racial to Post-Racial?: Reading and Reviewing *A Mercy* in the Age of Obama." MELUS 36.2 (summer 2011): 165-183. Cantiello discusses the misreading of Sorrow on the part of critics who attempt to place the enigmatic character within a black-white binary.

[3] "Toni Morrison Finds 'A Mercy' in Servitude." National Public Radio Author Interviews. All Things Considered. October 27, 2008.
http://www.npr.org/templates/story/story.php?storyId=96118766.

[4] Houston A. Baker, II, *Blues, Ideology, and Afro-American Literature: A Vernacular Theory* (Chicago: U of Chicago Press, 1984); Henry Louis Gates, II, *The Signifying Monkey: A Theory of African American Literary Criticism* (New York: Oxford U Press, 1988); Michael Awkward, *Inspiriting Influences: Tradition, Revision, and African American Women's Novels* (New York: Columbia U Press, 1989); Mae Gwendolyn Henderson, "Speaking in Tongues: Dialogics, Dialectics, and the Black Woman Writer's Literary Tradition." *Feminists Theorize the Political*. Judith Butler and Joan W. Scott, eds. (New York: Routledge, 1992): 144-166; and Cheryl Wall, *Worrying the Line: Black Women Writers, Lineage, and Tradition* (Chapel Hill: U of North Carolina Press, 2005).

[5] Cathleen Schandelmeier Bartels. "Toni Morrison's Discussion of *A Mercy*: An Experience for a Lifetime." *The NEIU Independent*. November 9, 2010.

[6] "Mama's Baby, Papa's Maybe: An American Grammar Book." *Diacritics* 17. 2 Culture and Countermemory: The "American" Connection (summer 1987): 64-81.

[7] *The Matrixial Borderspace* (Minneapolis: U of Minnesota P, 2006).

[8] See Mae Gwendolyn Henderson, *Borders, Boundaries, and Frames: Essays in Cultural Criticism and Cultural Studies* (New York: Routledge, 1995); bell hooks, *Yearning: Race, Gender, and Cultural Politics* (Boston: South End, 1990); Abdul JanMohamed, "Worldliness-Without World, Homelessness as Home: Toward a Definition of the Specular Border Intellectual." *Edward Said: A Critical Reader*, Michael Sprinkler, ed. (Cambridge: Blackwell, 1992); Paul Gilroy, *The Black Atlantic: Modernity and Double Consciousness* (Cambridge: Harvard U Press, 1992); Carol Boyce Davies, *Migrations of the Subject: Black Women, Writing, and Identity* (New York: Routledge, 1994); and Homi Bhabha, *The Location of Culture* (New York: Routledge, 2004).

[9] "Home." *The House That Race Built*. Wahneema Lubiano, ed. (New York: Random House, 1998): 3-12.

[10] "Structure, Sign, and Play in the Discourse of the Human Sciences." *Writing and Difference*, Alan Bass, translator (Chicago: U of Chicago P, 1978): 278-95.

[11] "Toni Morrison's Letter to Barack Obama," Tom McGeveran, *New York Observer*, January 28, 2008.

[12] The spring 2012 publication of Morrison's tenth novel *Home* and its narrative engagement with the 1950's Korean War through the perspective of the amnesiac, tormented veteran Frank "Smart" Money invite further critical reassessment of the author's evolving canon.

PART I:

'ARE YOU AFRAID?':
MERCIFUL HAUNTING
IN A NEW WORLD SETTING

CHAPTER ONE

"THESE CAREFUL WORDS … WILL TALK TO THEMSELVES": TEXTUAL REMAINS AND READER RESPONSIBILITY IN TONI MORRISON'S A MERCY

MARIA RICE BELLAMY

In many respects, Toni Morrison's *A Mercy* (2008) can be considered a prequel to her masterpiece, *Beloved* (1987). The action of *Beloved* occurs in the years just before and after the end of slavery, while *A Mercy* takes place during the era when slavery becomes entrenched and racialized in the colonies that will become the United States. In *Beloved,* an enslaved mother makes the unimaginable decision to kill her daughter rather than allow her to be raised in slavery, as the traumatic memories of the mother's enslavement and the presence of her dead daughter's ghost continue to haunt the elder woman. *A Mercy* portrays the aftermath of another enslaved mother's decision to offer her daughter in payment for her master's debt, hoping that a different master will give her daughter the chance of a better future. In this later text, however, it is the daughter who faces haunting memories of her mother's apparent rejection, while the mother, called *a minha mãe* (Portuguese for "my mother"), whose absence haunts the larger text, returns beyond space and time to deliver the explanatory monologue that closes the novel. Florens, the daughter, is never able to hear her mother's words, nor does her mother fully know the damage her decision causes her daughter. Instead, three centuries after this critical period in American history, it is the contemporary reader who is privy to both the reasoning of what one might call an abandoning parent and the torment of her abandoned child. Ultimately, Morrison positions her readers to reckon and receive these haunting remains.

My reading of this novel focuses on the figure of the abandoned child and the haunting presences that remain at the end of the text. First, *A Mercy* figures the entrance into slavery as a parent's abandonment of a child and indirectly explores the involvement of Africans in the process of enslaving other Africans. In this novel, Morrison portrays Florens' feelings of abandonment as well as her mother's memories of being taken from her home in Angola and having fellow Africans sell the mother into slavery. A broader reading of this text, however, requires us to recognize the multiplied forms of child abandonment in a period of tremendous social change, as early settlers explore the Americas and build new societies. The novel is thus populated with characters that have been cut loose from ties to kin and culture at an early age and struggle to define themselves and their place in the New World. While Morrison's characterizations of these abandoned children cross lines of race and gender, her special attention to Florens renders the additional level of devastation on the part of the African child in an increasingly racialized and hostile western society. Second, *A Mercy* ends with the physical, textual and ghostly remains of Florens' and her mother's traumatic experiences. Having survived the traumas of her youth and written a text that asserts her subjectivity, Florens remains alive at the novel's close, but the uncertainty of her future, in a society in which her status will become more rather than less precarious with time, haunts the reader. When the mother's ghostly intervention into the text answers Florens' desire to know the reason for the girl's abandonment, the reader of *A Mercy* is left with the knowledge that *a minha mãe* speaks to a daughter who is already lost to her and can never hear her words. Ultimately, the novel offers no assurance that Florens' written words, addressed to her estranged lover, or her mother's spoken words, directed toward Florens, will be received by their intended audiences. Their words remain, nevertheless, begging the questions: who *really* is the intended audience for their words and what are we, the readers, to do with these haunting presences? Morrison leaves them to haunt her contemporary readers and beckons us to receive them within ourselves to restore the personal and familial losses of American slavery.

The haunting presences in *A Mercy* link this text to a growing body of literature on contemporary forms of haunting, particularly in Ethnic American literature. Haunting serves primarily as a means of accessing lost or repressed knowledge, especially among subjugated peoples, whose history and culture is undervalued and under-recorded in mainstream American society. In her sociological study of haunting, Avery Gordon argues that "To write stories concerning exclusions and invisibilities is to write ghost stories" (17). The haunting aspect of these ghost stories relates to their ability to alter "the experience of being in time, the way we separate the past, the present and the future" and capture the multiplicity of connections that, in this case, enables a twenty-first century reader to be affected by the story of girl abandoned by her mother three centuries ago (Gordon xvi). In her recent study of haunting in African American literature and culture, Marisa Parham offers further nuance to this multiplicity of connections by analyzing the contemporary reader's internal response to external stimuli: "Being haunted means struggling with things that come to us from outside our discrete experiences of the world, but which we nonetheless experience as emerging out of our own psyches" (6). Haunting relates both to the collapse of time and the sensation that the experiences of a person from another time are our own because her experiences resonate with our own deep-seated cultural memory. This concept suggests Morrison's explanation of her own efforts to access her ancestral and cultural past and use the memories of others to gain "entrance into [her] own interior life" (Morrison "Site" 115). Morrison designs her novels to offer her readers a similar experience by providing them space to enter the text, allowing their personal memory and interior life to deepen and inform their reading. Finally, Gordon represents haunting as the haunted's experience with the agency of ghosts, whose "desires ... must be recognized'" (179). While Florens and her mother cannot make their intended audiences apprehend their narratives, they reach beyond the confines of the text to speak directly to the contemporary reader requiring us to hear, recognize, and affirm their stories. Their desire forces us to realize that "we are part of [their] story, for better or worse," and ghosts don't simply speak, they "speak to *me*" (Gordon 24, emphasis in original). In *A Mercy*, haunting figures of repressed knowledge encourage the reader to engage and respond to that knowledge.

A Mercy draws Morrison's readers into a different discursive space than many recent literary representations of haunting, including *Beloved*. In her exhaustive study of the genre she defines as contemporary narratives of cultural haunting, Kathleen Brogan argues that these texts "organize plots as a movement from negative to positive forms of haunting"[1] (17). Citing *Beloved,* she argues that "in giving narrative organization to Sethe's experience (the experience of the historical Margaret Garner and by extension, all victims of slavery), Morrison defines historical consciousness as a good form of haunting, in which the denied ghosts of the American past are finally integrated into America's national identity" (8). By implication, this process facilitates a release from traumatic repression and repetition, which we might call negative haunting. The expulsion of the ghost in *Beloved* offers some relief from this form of haunting, although the novel's end clearly suggests that neither Sethe nor her contemporaries are fully reconciled to their traumatic pasts or precluded from experiencing other subtler forms of haunting. The reader of *Beloved* is, nevertheless, left with the hope of Sethe recognizing herself as her own best thing and moving on to make a better life with (or without) Paul D. Morrison, however, leaves her readers with little sense of release or reason for hope at the end of *A Mercy*. As much as we would like the novel to organize and resolve Florens' and her mother's traumatic histories, these characters are left unsettled, with no true hope of creating better futures for themselves. For this reason, this novel has drawn criticism from some reviewers, including John Updike and Lenora Todaro, for its pessimism,[2] although some critics, including Waegner, have identified unfounded optimism. Neither pessimistic nor even guardedly optimistic, Morrison intentionally leaves her characters (and readers) in an unresolved middle space at the end of *A Mercy*.

From very different scholarly traditions, theologian Shelly Rambo and literary scholar Marisa Parham theorize this middle space, offering useful applications to our reading of *A Mercy*. In her theory of remaining, Rambo recognizes "a tenuous middle, in which both what is behind and what is ahead are unsettled and threatening and unknown" (Rambo "Redemption?" 109). Derived from the Greek word *menein,* meaning "to live on," remaining describes living on in the middle space after (and before) trauma "as a form of witness to the persistence of death in life" (Rambo "Haunted" 937). At the end of *A Mercy,* the reader recognizes that Florens' trials have not ended, that she and her descendants will live in bondage for generations without the hope of release. In Rambo's words, the moral of a text like *A Mercy* is one of "survival and witness, as opposed to … triumph through struggle" ("Redemption?" 112). Rambo's paradigm thus offers the possibility of imagining Florens as one who remains and lives on to witness survival in spite of the very real threat of future trauma.[3] Analyzing its pervasive rituals of mourning and remembrance, Parham characterizes African American culture as inhabiting a middle space between past and present, life and death. She considers such practices a "cultural imperative" requiring the contemporary African American to "remember events that are not [his] own and to testify to their otherwise un-witnessed effects," in other words "to choose to be haunted" (109). Describing haunting as "what it means to live in between things… to live with various forms of doubled consciousness," Parham invokes Du Bois' conception of double consciousness to situate the middle space of haunting as an implicit component of the African American experience (3). Thus, to be consciously African American requires being haunted, to "claim ownership" over another's experiences and wonder "what kind of responsibility might one have to this acquired knowledge?" (84, 8) Parham's question resonates with Morrison's readers who similarly wonder how to respond to *A Mercy*'s haunting elements and determine what responsibility we owe to the ghostly characters that remain at the novel's end. Morrison positions her readers to enter the middle space with her characters in order to heal the deep-seated wounds of slavery in the American consciousness.

In interviews Morrison has explained that she was drawn to writing about the colonial period in American history because of "how ad hoc everything was, how fluid and the unlikeliness, the unlikelihood of this nation becoming what it is" (Morrison "Bondage").[4] The undefined status of the American colonies mirrors the undefined and changeable status of the characters of *A Mercy*. Morrison explains, "everybody was for rent or for sale... particularly young people, children. They were motherless, fatherless... vulnerable" (Morrison "Bondage"). Without exception, Morrison's characters struggle to define themselves against experiences of abandonment, servitude or enslavement. The cast of characters in *A Mercy* enables Morrison to explore the possibilities and perils of self-definition in the beautiful and unforgiving New World landscape and imagine alternative versions of the American narrative of origin.

Of the characters in *A Mercy,* Jacob Vaark, Florens' new master, best represents the nascent American spirit of adventure and self-reliance, while his egalitarian ethos enables him to create a household modeling harmonious relations between the races represented in the colonies. The illegitimate child of a Dutchman and an English girl "of no consequence who died in childbirth," Vaark remembers well his life as an orphan in the streets of England, his stint in the poorhouse, and the series of fortunate events (including inheriting a patroonship in New Netherlands from a distant relative) that transformed "a ratty orphan" into a land owner (Morrison *A Mercy* 33, 12).[5] Traveling through "forests untouched since Noah, shorelines beautiful enough to bring tears," Vaark "relished never knowing what lay in his path... [and] flushed with pleasure when a crisis, large or small, needed invention and fast action" (12).[6] His embrace of the landscape and possibilities of the New World, tempered by his general disdain for slavery and sensitivity to the struggles of other abandoned children, positions Vaark to create and support an idealized New World family. He accepts Florens in partial payment of her master's debt, first, because he is "struck by the terror in her [mother's] eyes" and second, because he "found it hard to refuse when called on to rescue an unmoored, unwanted child" (26, 33). Vaark then brings her home to his motley crew of cast-off women: his wife Rebekka, whose father ships her from England to a stranger for the cost of her fare and being relieved of the responsibility "of feeding her" (74); Lina, a Native American woman, purchased as a servant from a Presbyterian couple who rescue her after her family is wiped out by small pox but reject her after she engages in what they deem immoral behavior; and Sorrow, a girl of uncertain origins whom Vaark receives from a sawyer simply looking to place her with someone "he trusted to do her no harm" (51). Forced to rely on each other in the untamed American frontier, this unlikely group forms "a kind of family" having "carved companionship out of isolation" (156). In the Vaark household, Morrison figures a New World Eden and offers one possible model for American race relations based on hybridity and mutual interdependence.[7]

Vaark's "rescue" of Florens, however, represents his first involvement with enslaved Africans and marks his development of the damning American trait of capitalist exploitation.[8] While visiting the plantation Jublio to settle his debt with its owner Senhor D'Ortega, Vaark becomes envious of his host's grand home, majestic wrought iron gate, and six children, particularly his two nearly grown sons. In spite of being sickened by D'Ortega's lavish home and ostentatious lifestyle, Vaark experiences a subtle shift in his ambitions, after leaving Jublio, first manifested in his decision to "look into" expanding his small trading operation into the more lucrative commerce in sugar and rum (32). Although this new line of business involves him in the slave-based Caribbean plantation economy, he reasons there to be "a profound difference between the intimacy of slave bodies at Jublio and a remote labor force in Barbados. Right? Right. He thought" (35). After his first concession, Vaark's fall is imminent. Though he has no heirs, having lost three sons in infancy and a daughter in a freak accident, Vaark becomes consumed with accumulating things, believing ownership to be his lasting legacy. Years later, when his wife asks why he wants to build their third home when they don't need it and have no one to inherit it, he answers what he has come to believe: "What a man leaves behind is what a man is" (89). Vaark ultimately comes to embody the Native American assessment of the European newcomers: "Cut loose from the earth's soul, they insisted on purchase of its soil, and like all orphans they were insatiable" (55).[9] Beyond his literal status as orphan, in his pursuit of ownership, Vaark loses his connection to the earth and brings damnation on himself. The ornate wrought iron gate with "two copper snakes" which Vaark builds as the entrance to his new home represents symbolically the infiltration of the serpent into the garden and becomes, in Lina's estimation, the entrance into "the world of the damned" (51). Vaark's death from small pox on the floor of his still uncompleted mansion articulates Morrison's condemnation of his choices and marks his expulsion from Eden. Indeed, the house which Vaark intends as a monument to his success becomes the manifestation of his folly, all that remains after his fall from grace and the destruction of the idyllic family that exists under his protection.

Jacob's decision to define himself according to an exploitative capitalist model results in his family's expulsion from paradise and leaves each woman vulnerable to the larger forces of their social environment. Babb argues that "The Vaark farm is laid waste by what dooms much in Morrison's work: adherence to egocentric individualism, isolation, and removal from community" (159). While Vaark's household provides a unique community for a time, his death destroys the unifying bond, leaving the women with nothing but isolation and remove from community. Lina notes that none of them are "attached to a church or recorded in its books, and without "some encircling outside thing" to define and protect their status, the women are outside of law, "illegal" (58). Morrison demonstrates, however, that it is the absence of traditional, particularly religious, structures that facilitates the Vaark household's idyllic community. After her husband's death and the loss of the "encircling" patriarchal structure of marriage, Rebekka aligns herself with the local Anabaptists, assuming and practicing their hierarchy and prejudices, including their belief that "Natives and Africans... had access to grace but not to heaven" (99). Her new loyalties destroy any remaining traces of Vaark's egalitarian ethos, and as the novel ends, the household is broken up as Rebekka prepares Florens for sale, seeks to give Sorrow away to whomever will take her, and subjects Lina to beatings and deprivations intended to civilize her.

While Vaark's process of self-definition presents an obvious contrast to the possibilities available to Florens, Morrison uses other captive female characters, including Lina and *a minha mãe*, to highlight the greater peril of Florens' situation. Unlike Lina, Florens does not have memories of a mother who dies struggling to care for her or of "[the] company of other children, industrious mothers in beautiful jewelry, the majestic plan of life; when to vacate, to harvest, to burn, to hunt" (50). Lina's childhood, steeped in a culture that provides her a defined role in a social order that gives her life meaning and purpose, enables her to endure the "solitude, regret and fury" that comes in her later years of captivity among the "Europes" (50, 54). After Vaark purchases her and following a disastrous and violent relationship with a European man and rejection by her Presbyterian guardians, Lina still manages "by piecing together scraps of what her mother had taught her before dying in agony" to construct "a way to be in the world" (48). Her self-definition incorporates useful elements from all parts of her past: "Relying on memory and her own resources, she cobbled together neglected rights, merged Europe medicine with native, scripture with lore" (48). Lina's process is characterized by inclusivity, recognition of what has been lost, and willingness to adapt to what has come. Babb compares Lina's synthesized belief system to "the syncretism of what would become United States culture" concluding that "*A Mercy* casts hybridity... as American fact" (158). In this way, Lina best represents the possibility for American cultural formation and offers an alternative to traditional narratives that emphasize the purity of American cultural origins. Finally, beginning her life in a setting characterized by purpose, dignity and wholeness, Lina does not lose her sense of self-worth, even as the world around her changes and becomes increasing hostile to her worldview.

Similarly, Florens' mother, in spite of suffering the traumas of capture, the Middle Passage, enslavement, and sexual exploitation, clearly remembers when her life as a woman of her clan and nation ends and her life as chattel begins. On a slave block in Barbados, *a minha mãe* has the shock of discovering that she "was not a person from [her] country, nor from [her] family. [She] was a negrita. Everything. Language, dress, gods, dance, habits, decoration, song—all of it cooked together in the color of [her] skin" (165). She witnesses herself as a raced object. Her birth, free in Angola, and her original formation as an African woman, however, enable her to see the violence of her situation in the larger context of the violence of patriarchal society. She explains that "men thrive on insults over cattle, women, water, crops" and understands warfare between her tribe and another as the beginning of her enslavement (163). Even on the slave ship she notices that the white sailors who take "pleasure to freshen us with a lash" also find it enjoyable "to lash their own" (164). *A minha mãe*'s broader range of experiences enables her to contextualize her situation and define her own worth in contrast to the role drawn for her in the New World economy. In contrast to Lina and *A minha mãe,* Florens never has the benefit of existing in a social structure that values her as a person with a meaningful role in society. Her life begins in enslavement, and the defining moments of her youth are scenes of rejection and abandonment.

Citing "the breakup of families" as "the monstrous thing that slavery in this country caused," Morrison intervenes in the earliest moment of slavery to represent the destruction of family bonds and Florens' experiences of rejection as the beginning of true bondage (Morrison "Bondage"). While a mother's love and acceptance normally form the foundation of a child's self-worth, *a minha mãe*'s abandonment becomes the negative basis of Florens' identity and makes her vulnerable to deeper levels of psychic bondage than Lina or her mother could imagine. First, Florens grows up with the haunting image of her mother, "standing hand in hand with her little boy," giving her away to a stranger but "saying something [she] cannot hear... something important" (3, 8). The pain of her mother's sending the girl away, when the mother keeps Florens' brother, is complicated further by the permanence of the separation, the cessation of communication with her mother, the loss of her love and guidance, and the inability ever to ask why. This experience creates a void in Florens which propels a desperate search for love and acceptance. In the Vaark household, Florens is "deeply grateful for every shred of affection, any pat on the head, any smile of approval" (61). For a time, she and Lina comfort the "Mother hunger—to be one or have one" from which they are both "reeling" (63); however, the appearance of a free man of color, the blacksmith who crafts Vaark's ornate gate, just as Florens enters adolescence, stimulates an overwhelming, blinding desire: "Nothing stops it. There is only you. Nothing outside of you. ... when at last our eyes hit I am not dead. For the first time I am live" (37, 38). Florens imagines the blacksmith as her "life and [her] security from harm, from any who look closely at [her] only to throw [her] away," seeing in him the satisfaction of her longing for intimate connection, release from bondage, and protection from future rejection (157). When Florens relives her original scene of rejection as the blacksmith appears to cast her aside in favor of a little boy, a foundling he takes into his custody after the boy's father or keeper's death, Florens becomes desperate, offering the blacksmith ownership of herself: "You alone own me" (141). Repelled by her self-objectification, the blacksmith casts Florens out of his presence, telling her to "Own yourself, Woman, and leave us be ... You are nothing but wilderness. No constraint. No mind" (141).[10] With this rejection Florens becomes unhinged, attacking both the boy and the man and discovering that what truly enslaves a person is on the inside: "it is the withering inside that enslaves and opens the door for what is wild" (160). This withering, the destruction of Florens' sense of her own humanity and worth, has its roots in her mother's rejection, is reinforced by the blacksmith's similar rejection, is fed by the brutalizing effects of racist discourse, and finally manifests itself in the wilderness of violence and self-hatred.

Morrison's concept of wilderness in *A Mercy* resonates with and expands on Stamp Paid's definition of the "jungle" in *Beloved* (198) and represents the second factor in Florens' descent into psychic bondage. Although white people believe the jungle to exist "under every dark skin," the jungle isn't naturally present in black people; rather it is planted in them by the objectification of white people and grows as blacks spend "their strength trying to convince [white people]... how human" they are (Morrison *Beloved* 198). Florens first feels the withering in her soul "in the Widow's closet" where witch-hunting villagers examined her to determine if she is "the Black Man's minion" (160, 113). Waegner, who usefully connects this encounter with Sethe's experiences with Schoolteacher, suggests that "Florens' humiliation" in the village inspires "her physical defense against the blacksmith's harsh words" just as Schoolteacher's study of Sethe's human and animal parts inspires her flight for freedom (100). In both cases white people seek to deconstruct the humanity of the black subject; however, rather than leading to a self-affirming stand against the blacksmith, I would argue that Florens' experience causes her to internalize another layer of rejection. Although she sees "No hate... or scare or disgust" in her observer's eyes, "[s]wine look at [her] with more connection when they raise their heads from the trough" (113). Montgomery suggests that this moment reveals the underlying "racist attitudes" through which Europeans viewed Africans before large-scale enslavement and which later justified perpetual enslavement (633). Cantiello further argues that the villager's inspection of Florens' body "resembles the treatment of slaves in a coffle" and is reminiscent of what "her mother [experiences] being sold in Barbados" (172). It is not surprising then that after escaping from the village, Florens knows she is "not the same" (115). She sees herself as "a thing apart," full of the exterior darkness she is born with and a new interior darkness she describes as "small, feathered, and toothy" (115). Unlike her mother who can separate her physical blackness from the readings projected on it, Florens internalizes racist discourse and wonders if the darkness within her is the source of her mother's rejection: "Is that what my mother knows? Why she chooses me to live without? Not the outside dark we share, a minha mãe and me, but the inside one we don't" (115). When the blacksmith rejects Florens for the wilderness he sees in her, the "feathered thing ... break[s] out on [the blacksmith]... wanting to tear [him] open the way" he tears her heart open (160). Florens' encounter with the villagers plants the jungle Stamp Paid speaks of and the wilderness the blacksmith identifies. The external threat to her humanity coupled with the rejection of the two people she loves and trusts to confirm her worth leads to Florens' violent and self destructive acts. In *A Mercy,* Morrison couples the profound dispossession of those born and reared in slavery, severed from meaningful kinship ties,[11] with the external objectification of racist discourse as the two-fold source of true psychic bondage.

In the aftermath of her two rejections and the breakdown of the fragile family model created in Vaark's home, Florens begins to write her personal narrative to discover a way to be in the world in which she lives. She addresses her story to the blacksmith and inscribes it on the walls of the abandoned home of her now deceased master (3). In this moment, she may be seen as countering what I would call the great discursive trauma of slavery: the individual being written out of a social and familial structure that imparts meaning and purpose to his existence and being re-written in western society as chattel, an object without the protection of familial or social structures. Florens' writing process becomes a dramatic representation of her asserting her subjectivity through narrative, using the master's words to create a counter-narrative to the objectifying discourse of western mercantilism, and establishing her history and physical body as living testaments to her survival in contrast to the dead home her master builds as a monument to his capitalist pursuits.

By the end of her narrative, Florens seems transformed from victim to fierce survivor. She begins her story with a markedly tentative, even conciliatory tone: "Don't be afraid. My telling can't hurt you in spite of what I have done and I promise to lie quietly in the dark—weeping perhaps or occasionally seeing the blood once more—but I will never again unfold my limbs to rise up and bear teeth" (3). In spite of any violence she may have directed toward the blacksmith and his ward, she begins her "confession" asking him not to fear her and promising to lie quietly and never again rise up against him (3). By the end of her narrative, however, she taunts the blacksmith: "Is that a tremble on your mouth, in your eye? Are you afraid? You should be" (157). Scully, a white indentured servant who often works for the Vaark's, observes the change in Florens after her encounter with the blacksmith, commenting that "the docile creature they knew had turned feral," her demeanor changing "from 'have me always' to 'don't touch me ever'" (146, 152). Waegner suggests that this change has made Florens "a strong woman who can perhaps find a way to avoid repeating her mother's experience of forced submission to the slave owner and loss of her daughter" (99). The well-documented vulnerability of the female slave affirms the unfounded optimism of this assessment. Instead, the shift from conciliatory to fierce marks Florens' recognition of her ability to inflict as well as receive pain and a determination to leave behind her girlish vulnerability. Her fearsome aspect, nevertheless, is complicated by her now ghostly presence. Scully again observes an unexplained haunting in the abandoned house, which the reader soon realizes is Florens haunting her master's house, as she scratches her story into the walls by candlelight: "Now, thirteen days later, the dead man had ... escaped his own grave. ... His glow began near midnight, floated for a while on the second story, disappeared, then moved ever so slowly from window to window" (144). Her haunting presence suggests Florens' in-between status at the end of the novel, no longer a vulnerable yet hopeful girl but not quite the strong, self-reliant woman she seeks to become. Whether conciliatory, fierce, or haunting, Florens ends her text with a declaration of her physical presence and survival: "I am also Florens" and "Slave. Free. I last" (161). Establishing her legacy as her ability to last, to survive the hard flames of her traumatic relationships and enslavement, Florens writes her story to define herself as a woman survivor and enter the written discourse of the New World.

Morrison, however, requires her readers to view the significance of Florens' narrative on more than one level. While contemporary readers may particularly desire to see Florens' text as liberatory, looking at it within the context of the novel and the history that surrounds it, we realize that Morrison complicates such a reassuring view, forcing us to ponder the actual value of the text Florens writes. The significance of her self-authorizing text is called into question because she defines herself in the terms of the blacksmith's and her mother's rejection of her and has no clear audience. First, Florens' constructed identity as a fierce woman includes her acceptance of the "wilderness" the blacksmith pronounces in her (157): "See? You are correct. A minha mãe too. I am become wilderness but I am also Florens. In full. Unforgiven. Unforgiving. No ruth, my love. None. Hear me?" (161) Conflating her two rejections, Florens assumes the identity she believes correlates with renunciation. The therapeutic value of Florens' narrative process is minimized as her writing does not result in a new understanding of herself or even a cathartic release. While she hopes her "telling will give [her] the tears [she] never [has]," it does not (158). Instead, she writes until her lamp runs out each night and sleeps among her words. Second, Florens nearly reaches the end of her written narrative before she remembers that her intended audience is illiterate. Thus, even if the blacksmith makes an unlikely return to the Vaark estate, he will not be able to read Florens' story. As Florens scratches the words using a nail on the walls of an abandoned home, we must wonder if the text is even legible. Realizing that her story will not reach its intended audience, Florens decides that her "careful words ... will talk to themselves" (161). Even as she continues to define herself in her mother and lover's terms, she declares her words to exist beyond writer and intended audience. Arguably, the words that have been her companions through the night have a life and meaning of their own, living on to haunt her master's house, whispering her story, contesting the values that have objectified her, and proclaiming her subjectivity. She finally imagines her words being set free when the house and all that it represents is consumed, possibly by a fire that she and Lina may set (161). Looking at the fuller text, the contemporary reader, the only being likely to know of their existence, becomes the inheritor of Florens' words as channeled through Morrison. While the fact that Florens writes her text may seem affirmation enough, even if she has no audience beyond herself and the words themselves, the reader is left to question the value of a text written into the vacuum in its own time and reckon with what it means to inherit the text centuries later.

Regardless of how we value her words, Florens' physical body must be reckoned with at the novel's end. As her mistress prepares to sell her, we are reminded that the physical body Florens claims in her text is also a commodity to be valued and sold. Her representation of her body reflects both what she believes her mother would want her to be and what slavery will require her to be. The young girl with the dismaying vice for shoes now emphasizes the hardness of her feet: "Mãe, you can have pleasure now because the soles of my feet are hard as cypress" (161). Cantiello suggests that Florens' "feet of a Portuguese lady" early in her life represent "her bodily resistance to complete enslavement" (171, quoting *A Mercy* 4). By implication Florens' movement from tender to hard feet marks her "trajectory to complete enslavement" (Cantiello 171). The hardness of her feet then becomes the physical manifestation of the internal reality both her psychic bondage and hardened heart. Although it declares her physical presence and determination to survive, *A Mercy* leaves Florens with a very uncertain future. Her impending sale portends her entrance into the larger world of slavery unprotected even by *a minha mãe*'s efforts to place her with a master who laughs at her too-small feet in broken-down adult shoes rather than leering at her fresh virginity (Waegner 93). While some readers may call Florens' survival and ability to tell her story a "tentative triumph," a more historically situated analysis of the text makes it difficult to imagine a happy ending for the story of a young female slave in 1690 (Waegner 110). The novel (and by extension its readers) is haunted by the history it precedes—two centuries of slavery and an additional century of legalized segregation of persons of African descent in the nation that would become the United States. Viewing Florens with the benefit of history, we know that she will need more than hard feet to endure the trials to come, that her descendants will experience more dehumanizing and destructive forms of bondage than she has, and that the coming redemption of her people is generations away and nearly unimaginable to her and her descendants in the midst of their suffering.

In a text structured around the absence of the mother and the nearly palpable desire to know the reason for her action, the unexpected return of *a minha mãe* in the closing section of *A Mercy* offers the other side of Florens' story and fills the implicit void in the text, even as it adds another layer of haunting. *A minha mãe*'s disembodied voice delivers her closing monologue to explain that the action her daughter understands as abandonment is actually "a mercy," meant to provide the possibility of a better life. Having experienced sexual abuse at the hands of her master and mistress as well as gang-rape by fellow slaves sent to "break" her when she first arrives at Jublio, *a minha mãe* tries to place her daughter in the care of a man who has "no animal in his heart" and will see Florens "as a human child, not pieces of eight" (165, 163, 166). Removing Florens from a place she knows to be dangerous, *a minha mãe* hopes that the pain of separation from her mother will be less damaging for Florens than the abuse she would suffer at Jublio. In *a minha mãe*'s verbal text Morrison explores the trauma of a parent who "has no control over what happens to [her] child" (Morrison "Bondage"). After kneeling in the dust imploring Vaark to take her daughter, *a minha mãe* declares that her heart remains in the dust "until you understand what I know and long to tell you" (167). The closing section suggests that the mother's desire to tell is as strong as the daughter's desire to know. While Morrison creates a space where these desires meet, she ultimately resists the urge "to make it possible for Florens to hear and know and understand why her mother gave her away... because the truth is, she would never know" (Morrison "Bondage"). Because the severing of familial ties in slavery was nearly always permanent, Morrison refuses Florens access to her mother's story, making her like the millions of other slaves who never know "who ... were their parents? Where were they?" (Morrison "Bondage"). The novel provides the reader the answers it denies Florens and leaves another haunting presence and text.

Ultimately, the reader receives the benefit both of Florens' story and her mother's disembodied words and feels most poignantly the loss her well-intentioned decision causes. We know that Florens' "one sadness" at the end of her story is never knowing what her mother wanted to tell her and never having the opportunity to show her mother that she has become a tough woman with hard feet (161). We also know what *a minha mãe* wishes for Florens to understand: "to be give dominion over another is a hard thing; to wrest dominion over another is a wrong thing; to give dominion of yourself to another is a wicked thing. Oh Florens. My love.

Hear a tua mãe" (167). By the novel's end, we apprehend the distance
between Florens' perceptions of and her mother's actual hopes for her.
With the benefit of her mother's wisdom, Florens might have recognized
the corruption sown in Vaark's soul after he is given dominion over
others, the evil of D'Ortega wresting dominion over others, and the
abomination of offering the blacksmith dominion over herself. Never
knowing the depth of her mother's love and good intentions, Florens
receives and internalizes rejection and wilderness as her mother's legacy
to her and imagines her mother being pleased by her hard feet and heart.[12]

Finally, the contemporary reader's responsibility to these characters
and their ghostly remains is to receive and honor them. Reading *a minha
mãe*'s story as "both a retelling of history and a 'rememory,' to borrow
Morrison's term," Babb suggests that her memories and Florens' "are the
only bonds available to a mother and daughter caught in the reality of
slavery" (155, 156). While I would argue that Morrison offers *a minha
mãe* and Florens not even this intangible connection, the concept of
rememory as memory that exists "in the world... floating around out there
outside [the rememberer's] head," seems an appropriate metaphor for both
a minha mãe's spoken narrative and Florens' written narrative (Morrison
Beloved 36). The existence of these texts in the world, separate from their
creators, facilitates Morrison's channeling of their words in her novel and
offers her readers the opportunity to "go there and stand in the place where
it was [so that] it will happen again" (Morrison *Beloved* 36). Entering into
this space of rememory, the twenty-first century reader relives *a minha
mãe* and Florens' experiences. The reading process then becomes "a kind
of memory-work" such that "our encounters with texts work on us, work
us over, make us remainders of them" (Parham 5). Here we imagine the
text imprinting the reader, imparting some of its ghostliness to us. Thus,
we become Florens, the lost child, and hear *my mother* speaking words of
love. We become the mother speaking love to other lost children. The
contemporary reader then becomes the bridge across the chasm that
separates mother and child and holds them in the love they could not share
with each other, thus healing their tormented souls.

New World black readers receive with Florens the answers to the deep-
seated questions within our own cultural memory about who our ancestors
are, who sold them and who abandoned them, and a level of our cultural
pain is healed. Certainly, of course, this text does not speak only to black
readers. As Gordon notes in her chapter on *Beloved,* "Morrison's call for
accountability suggests that it is our responsibility to recognize just where
we are in the story, even if we do not want to be there" (188). Morrison's
numerous and varied portrayals of abandoned children in colonial America

enable her readers to find many possible versions of their ancestral selves and carry other narratives of repressed history to the present day. Babb argues that "the image of [Florens'] expansive words confined reflects the necessity for augmented origins stories. Narrative space must be made for those voices that once talked to and for themselves but have been muted by the historical record" (159). Through Morrison's novel, the contemporary reader recovers lost ancestors, inscribes alternative narratives of origin, and brings healing to unresolved traumas.

Morrison, nevertheless, leaves the characters and readers of *A Mercy* in the haunted middle space of survival and witness. Although unable to know what becomes of mother or daughter, we are their witnesses in the current era. What sustenance we find at the close of this text is the revelation of the abandoning mother's love for her child, which, reminiscent of the inscription to *Beloved*, calls "her beloved, which was not beloved" (*ix*). As the inheritors of *a minha mãe*'s narrative, the contemporary reader receives her love, mourns her loss, and remains haunted. In Rambo's words, she remains "the haunting figure of love… seeking forms of life that are not necessarily triumphant but nonetheless sustaining" ("Haunted" 940). Finally, through her haunting figures and texts, Morrison enables her readers to hear and share the call of love.

Notes

[1] See Brogan 1-11 for a thorough explanation of the characteristics of this genre and how it differs from previous literary forms of haunting in the gothic tradition.

[2] Updike writes in his review of *A Mercy* that "a betranced pessimism saps [Morrison's] plot of the urgency that hope imparts to human adventures." Similarly, Todaro calls *A Mercy* "a sad pessimistic novel."

[3] Rambo's theory of remaining, based on her reading of the Gospel of John with its closing affirmations of love and haunting remains, seeks to address the questions: what does it mean to survive (remain) after death (or trauma) and what does it mean for the gospel text to remain and be transmitted? While it may seem questionable to read Morrison's novel through a theological paradigm considering her thorough critique of various church traditions in *A Mercy,* Morrison's criticism is generally directed toward hypocritical and oppressive religious institutions rather than simpler and more organic forms of spirituality. Further, her broad use of biblical and classical allusions offers many opportunities to analyze the tropes and metaphors of the Judeo-Christian tradition represented in various forms in her novels. Finally, Rambo's theory of remaining carefully revises the "triumphalism" of many contemporary religious doctrines to consider how "trauma … interrupts any theology that would leap right from the crucifixions of history to the hope of resurrection" (Keller *ix*). Rambo instead restores the middle space between Christ's death and resurrection as the space in which most of us live and which

"inspires an interhuman capacity to stand by each other in our sufferings—especially those who cannot be victoriously fixed" (Keller *x*). Rambo's theory provides a useful middle space in which to consider traumas not easily resolved.

[4] See Jennings' review of *A Mercy* for a fuller discussion of the novel's historical context and the legal, social and economic developments of the time period that establish the structure of American society and determine the fate of enslaved Africans.

[5] Henceforth, I will simply use the page number to indicate quotations from *A Mercy*.

[6] In spite of his description of forests "untouched since Noah," Vaark originally recognizes the rights of Native tribes "to whom it all belonged" over the endless succession of claims to the land by churches, companies and other European institutions (12-13). On his way to Jublio to discuss a bad debt, he travels native trails "mindful of their maize fields, careful through their hunting grounds, politely asking permission to enter a small village here, a larger one there" (13). His initial sensitivity is later overwhelmed by greed.

[7] See Gates' review of the novel for a broader discussion of its pastoral elements.

[8] Babb notes that beginning her novel with a trader travelling through Virginia, Morrison "decentraliz[es] the rhetoric of New England religious mission" to reveal the commercial origins of many American settlements, including Virginia and New Netherlands (151).

[9] Lina laments further that the home's construction requires "the death of fifty trees" which Vaark replaces "with a profane monument to himself" (43: 44). These actions demonstrate the end of his original sensitivity to the land and Native claims to it. Waegner characterizes Vaark's pursuit of wealth and ownership as a "New World Faustian pact with the devil" (95).

[10] Babb argues that "the blacksmith's rejection of Florens might stem from both his contempt for her blind devotion and his fear that too close an approximation to her enslavement jeopardizes his own liberty.... For his own social survival he must maintain a clear demarcation between his free blackness and Florens' enslaved blackness" (154).

[11] In "Mama's Baby, Papa's Maybe," Spillers explores how the system of slavery obliterated traditional kinship structures, leaving the enslaved orphaned and unprotected. She notes that under the slave system, "the offspring of the female [slave] does not 'belong' to the Mother, [and] is [not] 'related' to the 'owner'" (Spillers 395); thus, "The offspring of the enslaved, 'being unrelated both to their begetters and to their owners... find themselves in the situation of being orphans'" (Spillers 396).

[12] While the presumed rejection by her mother is what most traumatizes Florens, destruction of this connection is not the only loss slavery causes her. Neither she nor her mother will ever know the identity of her father because she is conceived as a result of gang rape. Morrison demonstrates forcefully that the violence of slavery destroys the family at every level.

Works Cited

Babb, Valerie. *"E Pluribus Unum?*: The American Origins Narrative in Toni Morrison's *A Mercy. MELUS* 36 (2) (2011): 147–164. Print.

Brogan, Kathleen. *Cultural Haunting: Ghosts and Ethnicity in Recent American Literature.* Charlottesville: UP of Virginia, 1998. Print.

Cantiello, Jessica Wells. "From Pre-Racial to Post Racial?: Reading and Reviewing *A Mercy* in the Age of Obama." *MELUS* 36 (2) (2011): 165–183. Print.

Gates, David. "Original Sins." Rev. of *A Mercy* by Toni Morrison. *New York Times* November 30, 2008. Web. *nytimes.com* (accessed November 29, 2009).

Gordon, Avery F. *Ghostly Matters: Haunting and the Sociological Imagination.* Minneapolis: U of Minnesota Press, 1997. Print.

Jennings, La Vinia Delois. "*A Mercy:* Toni Morrison Plots the Formation of Racial Slavery in Seventeenth-Century America." Rev. of *A Mercy* by Toni Morrison. *Callaloo* 32 (2) (2009): 645–703. Web. *Project Muse* (accessed November 1, 2009).

Keller, Catherine. Foreword. *Spirit and Trauma: A Theology of Remaining.* By Shelly Rambo. Louisville: Westminster John Knox Press, 2010. *ix-xi.* Print.

Morrison, Toni. *A Mercy.* New York: Knopf-Random House, 2008. Print.

—. *Beloved.* 1987. New York: Plume-Penguin, 1988. Print.

—. "Toni Morrison on Bondage and A Post-Racial Age." Interview with Michel Martin. *Tell Me More.* National Public Radio. 10 Dec. 2008. Radio. Transcript. http://www.npr.org/templates/story/story.php?storyId=98072491

—. "The Site of Memory." *Inventing the Truth: The Art and Craft of Memoir.* Ed. William Zinssner. Boston: Houghton-Mifflin, 1987. Print.

Montgomery, Maxine. "Got on My Traveling Shoes: Migration, Exile, and Home in Toni Morrison's *A Mercy.*" *Journal of Black Studies* 42 (4) (2011): 627–637. Print.

Parham, Marisa. *Haunting and Displacement in African American Literature and Culture.* New York: Routledge, 2009. Print.

Rambo, Shelly. "Beyond Redemption?: Reading Cormac McCarthy's *The Road* after the End of the World." *Studies in the Literary Imagination* 41 (2) (2008): 99–120. Print.

—. "Haunted (by the) Gospel: Theology, Trauma, and Literary Theory in the Twenty-First Century." *PMLA* 125 (4) (2010): 936–941. Print.

Spillers, Hortense. "Mama's Baby, Papa's Maybe: An American Grammar Book." In *Feminisms: An Anthology of Literary Theory and Criticism,* ed. Rosalyn Warhol & Diane Herudl, 384–405. New Brunswick: Rutgers UP, 1997. Print.

Todaro, Lenora. "Toni Morrison's *A Mercy*: Racism Creation Myth." Rev. of *A Mercy* by Toni Morrison. *The Village Voice* November 19, 2008. Web. *villagevoice.com* (accessed February 18, 2011).

Updike, John. "Dreamy Wilderness: Unmastered Women in Colonial Virginia." Rev. of *A Mercy* by Toni Morrison. *The New Yorker* November 3, 2008. Web. *Newyorker.com* (accessed February 18, 2011).

Waegner, Cathy Covell. "Ruthless Epic Footsteps: Shoes, Migrants and the Settlement of the Americas in Toni Morrison's *A Mercy*." In *Post-National Enquiries: Essays on Ethnic and Racial Border Crossings*, ed. Jopi Nyman, 91–112. Newcastle upon Tyne: Cambridge Scholars Press, 2009. Print.

PART II:

'A SLAVE BY CHOICE':
RE-READING THE (NEO) SLAVE NARRATIVE

CHAPTER TWO

THE (NEO) SLAVE NARRATIVE IN BLACK AND WHITE: TONI MORRISON'S RE-ENVISIONING OF MASCULINITY IN *A MERCY*

GENE MELTON, II

> Softly, suddenly, it began to snow, like a present come down from the sky. Sethe opened her eyes to it and said, "Mercy." And it seemed to Paul D that it was—a little mercy—something given to them on purpose to mark what they were feeling so they would remember it later on when they needed to.
>
> —Toni Morrison, *Beloved* (152)

Toni Morrison's *A Mercy* is set in the late seventeenth century at a time when the transatlantic slave trade had become instantiated as a general global reality and when slavery was becoming increasingly codified in and integral to the social, economic and political environment of everyday life for citizens of the English colonies on the North American continent in particular. Structurally, the novel presents half of its narrative as chapters told exclusively from the first-person perspective of Florens, a female African slave, who spends most of the novel travelling on foot to find the blacksmith, who has been her lover, to bring him back to Jacob Vaark's plantation to heal his widow, her mistress. Alternating with the Florens chapters are episodes contained in chapters told from the third-person perspective of various other characters (male, female, black, white and Native American) and that comment upon and further flesh out the setting, current plot and historical background for the action of the story. A final chapter is told from the first-person perspective of Florens' mother who explains in those closing pages her rationale for choosing to send Florens and not her younger brother away with Vaark, the primary slaveholder in the novel; really a coda to the piece, this chapter resolves the psychological conflict at the heart of Florens' struggle to define herself in relation to the events of her life and her experience of herself as nothing—a non-entity under the domination of others who have greater agency and who have access to the power to assert that agency.

To be sure, the elements of *A Mercy* that place it within the conventional paradigm of the (neo) slave narrative circulate most precisely around the African (and Native American) female characters. Although an image of the individual whose narrative this was, a title-page assertion of authorship, supporting testimonials by whites, a verse serving as an epigraph and (variously) material appended after the narrative to document further the narrator-author's enslavement or to comment further on the evils of slavery and the merits of the abolitionist cause (Olney 152–153)— the para-textual material that slave narratives usually included—do not appear in *A Mercy*, while most of the other features of the slave narrative are accounted for in Morrison's short novel. Indeed, of the twelve components of the "actual narrative" to be found in most (if not all) nineteenth-century slave narratives that James Olney has schematized (152–153), most are evident in the "confession" (itself a component of the tradition) that Florens provides in detailing her history and in recording the events of her journey to find the blacksmith. In the overall narrative, for instance, we begin with the standard glance toward nativity and imprecise knowledge of paternity for the primary character, Florens: a cruel master appears, in the person of D'Ortega, the plantation owner who trades Florens to pay his debt to Vaark; an "extraordinarily strong, hardworking slave" emerges in the person of Lina (although, as a Native American, she is thus not the "pure African" [153] Olney says this figure often is); a white "Reverend Father" (*A Mercy* 6) violates the law and teaches Florens, her mother and her brother how to read and write; other enthusiastic, if hypocritical Christians give Florens shelter as she makes her dangerous journey away from the plantation, and strike fear into her with their odd rituals and potential for betrayal, for even though this journey is sanctioned, Florens still risks all the dangers of a fugitive slave; another female character, Sorrow, changes her name once she has given birth; and, throughout the novel, various characters offer the direct and indirect "reflections on slavery" that Olney also finds prevalent in nineteenth-century slave narratives (153).

Indeed, in "Enslavements," her 2008 *New Republic* review of *A Mercy*, Ruth Franklin describes the book as "a slender novel that plunges resoundingly into the pre-history of black America to tell the interlocking stories of three slavewomen and their mistress," and she finds the story "as linguistically rich and emotionally wrenching as [Morrison's] best work of the 1970s and 1980s" (36). As in all of her writing about slavery, epitomized by her novel *Beloved*, Franklin says that Morrison here is again "using [slavery] as a metaphor for the *female* condition" (37, emphasis added). Objecting to the "vaguely ideological" feeling she perceives in Morrison's choosing "to tell the stories of mothers, not fathers" (39), Franklin concludes that until Morrison broadens the scope of her narrative vision, her work will be problematically gendered:

> As long as she uses her lyrical and tormented novels as vehicles for the insistence on man's inhumanity to woman, her artistic achievement will continue to be interrupted by the testimonial groan. The bits and pieces of life should not be dominated by the grinding of the ax. (39)[1]

While, like Franklin, I find much in *A Mercy* that harkens back to *Beloved* and to other fiction in Morrison's earlier body of work, I also find much in the novel that indicates another way of considering Morrison's particular narrative emphases, a way that—in stark contradiction to Franklin's reading of the book—provides for a significant presence of men in the story.[2]

-II-

Although *A Mercy*, like *Beloved*, centers on a female character's literal and psychological journey, the more recent novel also expands, in its non-Florens chapters, to also contemplate the masculine experience of a world in which slavery is a fact of life, and does so in a way that complicates the notion of perpetrators and victims in this system. Many white males hold slaves to be sure, but—the story reveals—some, like Jacob Vaark, are not always comfortable with the power that role gives them. Other white men, like Scully and Willard, find themselves, as indentured servants, no better off culturally, economically and legally than most African slaves. And in the case of the blacksmith, Morrison presents a powerful, self-actualized figure of a black man in colonial America who is not a slave and, because of the late seventeenth-century timeframe of the novel and the still relatively nascent instantiation of the slave culture in the colonies, has never been a slave.

For the purposes of this discussion, then, I shall focus on these four main male characters in the novel—one black, the other three white—to examine how *A Mercy* continues—ironically, as a (neo) slave narrative—the critical project Morrison proposes in *Playing in the Dark: Whiteness and the Literary Imagination*, her celebrated reflections on American literature. "My project," Morrison asserts in *Playing in the Dark*, "is an effort to avert the critical gaze from the racial object to the racial subject;

from the described and imagined to the describers and imaginers; from the serving to the served" (90). Indeed, through her interweaving of multiple third-person perspectives in the non-Florens chapters of the book, Morrison once again adapts the genre of the (neo) slave narrative, a form that she masterfully transforms in her earlier novel *Beloved*, so that in *A Mercy* it allows for a generous reconsideration of the nature of black *and* white masculinity during the early period of Africans' enslavement in North America.

Perhaps the great irony of *A Mercy* as a (neo) slave narrative is that the only male in the book who is, from the start, truly at liberty—socially and psychologically—is the blacksmith, a man of African descent who is "a free man," one who has "rights ... and privileges, like Sir [Vaark]. He could marry, own things, travel, sell his own labor" (*A Mercy* 45). As Lina, a Native American servant in the Vaark household, observes, the blacksmith is a potentially dangerous figure. He exhibits, Lina notes, a certain "arrogance" that leads him, without apology or reticence, to do "something she had never seen an African do: he looked directly at Mistress, lowering his glance, for he was very tall, never blinking those eyes slanted and yellow as a ram's" (*A Mercy* 45). In making this direct eye-contact, the blacksmith alters Lina's understanding of what might be possible in a social interaction with an African: "It was not true, then, what she had heard; that for them [Africans] only children and loved ones could be looked in the eye; for all others it was disrespect or a threat" (*A Mercy* 45). The blacksmith is, indeed, a witness to the "slaves freer than free men" that he himself will assert, late in the novel, as a reality that Florens should come to accept (*A Mercy* 160).

From his first appearance, the blacksmith is a transformative figure. Indeed, the blacksmith enters the story to provide skilled labor in the construction of the third—and grandest—incarnation of the master's home on Jacob Vaark's Maryland plantation. In particular, he is commissioned to craft the ironwork gate that—like similar gates to Heaven, Hell and Eden imagined in such a popular seventeenth-century representation of the quintessential Christian creation myth as Milton's *Paradise Lost*[3]— provides a barrier against unauthorized entrance into or egress from the Vaark property. In keeping with the Edenic iconography, the barrier the blacksmith produces is beautiful, "wondrous to see" (*A Mercy* 36), but is also a "sinister gate" (51) that symbolizes potential dangers, potential temptations evocative of the Biblical archetypes, in the "glittering cobras" that "kiss at [its] crown" (*A Mercy* 36).

Like the gate, and very much like Cholly Breedlove from *The Bluest Eye*, Morrison's first novel, the blacksmith is a figure alternately divine and demonic. He is a healer, "a savior" (*A Mercy* 127), but his methods are extravagant and frightening, aligning him as much with magic as with miracles. When Sorrow, a servant of Irish descent living on the Vaark plantation, is burned, the blacksmith treats her with vinegar and her own blood in a ritual manner that recalls communion and cannibalism, sacrifice and exorcism:

> ... the smithy called for vinegar. Lina went to fetch it, and when it came, he doused Sorrow's boils and the skin of her face and arms, sending her into spasms of pain. While the women sucked air and Sir frowned, the blacksmith heated a knife and slit open one of the swellings. They watched in silence as he tipped Sorrow's own blood drops between her lips. (*A Mercy* 125)

As Alan Rice has argued, in his analysis of her metaphorical depiction of cannibalistic activity in *Beloved*, we must be mindful of the "historical and avowedly Atlanticist context" (107) of Morrison's use of that trope. In several scenes in *Beloved*, Rice asserts, Morrison "reverses the stereotype of black bloodthirstiness by showing the actual bloodthirsty character of the white racists" (117). Compared to the ritual blood-letting and other forms of physical abuse enacted by white Christians that Florens witnesses during her travels,[4] the Blacksmith's actions in this scene from *A Mercy* similarly transform the implications of the potential cannibalism here. The African ritual is creative, not destructive, and is a remedy for an individual and communal body injured by increasingly diseased European cultural practices. In performing this ritual, then, the Blacksmith confirms his potency, to be sure, but—more importantly—he also demonstrates that he has not lost the vital connection to an African heritage that provides him with both a coherence of personal identity and a power to heal others in the larger communities he graces with his temporary presence.

In addition to his capacity as a healer, the blacksmith is also a god-like creator, an artist who shapes from base materials works of great beauty. His work, however, requires him to labor in fire, and that associates him with Hell and the alchemy of potentially forbidden admixtures. The blacksmith's physical being likewise evokes this archetypal tension between fire and freedom, power and production, as Florens records in one of her early chapters:

> The first time I see it you are shaping fire with bellows. The shine of water runs down your spine and I have shock at myself for wanting to lick there. I run away into the cowshed to stop this thing from happening inside me. Nothing stops it. There is only you. Nothing outside of you. My eyes not my stomach are the hungry parts of me. There will never be enough time to

look how you move. Your arm goes up to strike iron. You drop to one knee. You bend. You stop to pour water first on the iron then down your throat. Before you know I am in the world I am already kill by you. My mouth is open, my legs go softly and the heart is stretching to break. (*A Mercy* 38-39)

When Florens acts on her desire, surrendering to the blacksmith not only with her heart and mind but also with her body, the moment is rendered by Sorrow as an energetic pastoral "dance":

This here female stretched, kicked her heels and whipped her head left, right, to, fro. It was a dancing. Florens rolled and twisted from her back to his. He hoisted her up against the hickory; she bent her head into his shoulder. A dancing. Horizontal one minute, another minute vertical. (*A Mercy* 128)

In this "silent submission" upon the grass beneath a tree, moreover, we have lovers described in terms of the coupling of snakes, an image that recalls not only the wrought-iron artistry of the gate, the symbol of the blacksmith's talent and labor, but also the underlying Christian myth of the fall of Eve that his presence both invokes and challenges. More profoundly still, it is not unimportant that it is iron that the blacksmith works into an expression of his identity as an artist and as a man—the iron does not shackle or silence him, the way the chains of the coffle or the metal of a bit are used to control and contain Paul D and other black men in *Beloved*.

Morrison complicates the character of the blacksmith still further in his final appearance in the novel, a scene that—in its essential tragedy—has some parallels to the narrative in *Beloved*. Her journey complete, Florens finds the blacksmith and secures his help in treating Rebekka, Vaark's widow. While he is away tending to this task, however, Florens finds herself taking care of the young boy he has adopted since she last saw him; jealous that this child might divert the blacksmith's attention from her, Florens injures the boy. When he learns of this, the blacksmith strikes Florens and insists that she leave his home. Such behavior suggests a different paradigm of masculinity for the blacksmith, one that makes him more like the violent, abusive men we see in other of Morrison's works, such as Paul D who responds with emotional and physical aggression in *Beloved*. Despite this moment of aggression, though, the blacksmith still proves to be one of the most enlightened figures in the novel as he explains to Florens how and why she continues to be a slave of her own making:

> Sir makes me that [a slave].
> I don't mean him.
> Then who?
> You.
> What is your meaning? I am a slave because Sir trades for me.
> No. You have become one. (*A Mercy* 141)

The blacksmith thus can utter, with harsh, godlike judgment, both his testament and his commandment: "Own yourself, woman, and leave us be" (*A Mercy* 141).

But as he is very much a man, the blacksmith is also subject to retaliation—Florens strikes him with his own tongs, leaving him to "stagger and bleed" (158) as she makes her way home. And in this moment we see that he shares with "a minha mãe"[5] the terrible burden of providing the painful, all-too-human salvation Florens needs. Like a minha mãe's sacrifice years before, the blacksmith's necessary rejection of Florens here "was not a miracle. Bestowed by God. It was a mercy. Offered by a human" (*A Mercy* 166–167).

Thus the blacksmith is a vital, if enigmatic, figure; one who serves to inspire some characters and to challenge others. As such, he becomes the essential "disrupting darkness" (91) to which Morrison calls for greater attention in *Playing in the Dark*, and—indeed—she speaks of the blacksmith in terms that confirm for readers that she wants him equated with that trope: "So Lina knew she was the only one alert to the breakdown stealing toward them. The only one who foresaw the disruption, the shattering a free black man would cause" (*A Mercy* 61).

Just as Morrison makes her portrait of the blacksmith neither wholly positive nor wholly negative, so too does she make Jacob Vaark a complex character, rather than the stereotypically brutal slave owner one might expect of the slave narrative tradition. In fact, Morrison makes clear that "flesh was not his commodity" (*A Mercy* 22).

A man interested in travel more than in farming or managing a plantation, Vaark finds himself participating reluctantly in that culture despite himself. When the novel opens he is travelling for his company to collect on a debt from D'Ortega, an aristocratic (if ultimately broke) landowner and slaveholder, who has lost an entire cargo of slaves due to his own arrogant mismanagement of his business concerns. At once disgusted by D'Ortega, whom he considers merely a "substitute for a man" (*A Mercy* 26), Vaark misses no opportunity to criticize what the aristocrat represents. D'Ortega's Catholicism sets him apart from Vaark, a Protestant, but the repulsion stems from something deeper, more essential. Vaark perceives "something sordid and overripe" in D'Ortega, and finds even his speech offensive; there is something "sly, indirect, instead of straight and manly," he believes, in the way D'Ortega converses (*A Mercy* 23). In addition, Vaark notes that D'Ortega's very physical presence embodies something to be wary of: "he believed the set of that jaw, the drooping lids, hid something soft, as if his hands, accustomed to reins, whips and lace, had never held a plow or axed a tree" (*A Mercy* 23). In short, this is a man Vaark desperately does not want to be.

And yet, Morrison also makes us aware that—despite his distaste for D'Ortega as a man and a representative of the aristocratic class—Vaark nevertheless envies D'Ortega his status and the trappings of success. In fact, Vaark plans to imitate, with modifications, the architectural features of Jublio, D'Ortega's plantation, when he returns to his own home. In doing so, he essentially founds, like God, his own form of Eden and, like Satan, its opposite—his own form of Pandemonium:

> So mighten it be nice to have such a fence to enclose the headstones in his own meadow? And one day, not too far away, to build a house that size on his own property? On that rise in back, with a better prospect of the hills and the valley between them? Not as ornate as D'Ortega's. None of that pagan excess, of course, but fair. And pure, noble even, because it would not be compromised as Jublio was. (*A Mercy* 27)

The difference, however, is that Vaark will not found his "empire" on the backs of slave labor; an ambitious white man, he hopes to forge a new way to success:

> Jacob sneered at wealth dependent on a captured workforce that required more force to maintain. Thin as they were, the dregs of his kind of Protestantism recoiled at whips, chains and armed overseers. He was determined to prove that his own industry could amass the fortune, the station D'Ortega claimed without trading his conscience for coin. (*A Mercy* 28)

This fiscal, political, religious and social policy also extends to his treatment of Florens, whom he finally accepts as payment of D'Ortega's debt. Unlike the traditional slave holder portrayed in many slave narratives, including Morrison's *Beloved*, Vaark makes no sexual demands on Florens, and nor does he force himself upon Lina or Sorrow, the other bondswomen he and his wife have brought into their home.

In addition, Vaark differs from other landed, slave-owning white men in the community in that, as Lina observes, he "behaved as though the blacksmith was his brother" (*A Mercy* 60). Morrison continues to describe their interaction from Lina's perspective:

Lina had seen them bending their heads over lines drawn in dirt. Another time she saw Sir slice a green apple, his left boot raised on a rock, his mouth working along with his hands; the smithy nodding, looking intently at his employer. Then Sir, as nonchalantly as you please, tipped a slice of apple on his knife and offered it to the blacksmith who, just as nonchalantly, took it and put it in his mouth. (*A Mercy* 60-61)

What is most compelling in this depiction of the relationship between these two men—one white, the other black; one European, the other African; both free—is their shared nonchalance. They respect one another as fellow men, as fellow human beings. In this exchange, the knife is a utensil for shared consumption, not a weapon for enforced domination. That they commune over pieces of apple in a doomed Eden, however, underscores the tenuousness and temporariness of this homo-social bond. Indeed, in *Beloved*, set two centuries later, such a nonchalant sharing between black and white men is impossible; in the chain-gang scene, for example, the transformation of this casual communion into an oppressive display of white racial empowerment is absolute—in word as well as in deed:

Chain up completed, they [the black male prisoners] knelt down ... Kneeling in the mist they waited for the whim of a guard, or two or three. Or maybe all of them wanted it. Wanted it from one prisoner in particular or none—or all.

"Breakfast? Want some breakfast, nigger?"
"Yes, sir."
"Hungry, nigger?"
"Yes, sir."
"Here you go."

Occasionally a kneeling man chose gunshot in his head as the price, maybe, of taking a bit of foreskin with him to Jesus ... (*Beloved* 127)

Thus, this complete breakdown in relations between black and white men, as Nathan Grant and Darieck Scott have recently observed in their analyses of the abuse Paul D and the other black inmates suffer at the hands of the prison guards in *Beloved*, will lead inevitably to a system of racist, classist patriarchy that permits and, indeed, encourages privileged white men to indulge in the rape not only of women, but also of other, less privileged men. As if presaging this outcome, Vaark's demise, before his grand mansion is complete, further confirms Lina's fear of the "breakdown stealing toward" the surviving members of the Vaark plantation and the colonial community at large.

In addition to the blacksmith, who complicates the figure of the free African male, and Jacob Vaark, who accepts the blacksmith as an equal and otherwise challenges assumptions about the motivations and goals of the slaveholder, the inclusion of Scully and Willard, two white men who are indentured servants, as fully realized minor characters allows Morrison to complicate still further her (neo) slave narrative's depiction of raced masculinity. That these two indentured white men also engage in sexual activity (if not a fully realized romantic relationship) with one another further separates them from the empowerment that was (and, largely, still is) the hegemonic purview of economically and socially privileged white males who espouse what we today consider a heterosexual paradigm. In some ways, then, these two figures offer the most striking revision to the slave narrative, as they open the form to a fuller contemplation of ways in which African slavery was but one part of a much larger institutionalization of oppressive labor policies and social constraints operating in the English colonies on the North American continent.

Indeed, the New World in *A Mercy* is a problematic Eden for both slaves and indentured servants, a depiction that would not have been unfamiliar to seventeenth-century writers and readers of discourse on the Americas. In "Freedom, Service, and the Trade in Slaves: The Problem of Labour in *Paradise Lost*," Maureen Quilligan provides a succinct overview of indentured servitude as she argues that, in *Paradise Lost*'s focus on labor, Milton ultimately renders Eden as the New World anxiously awaiting the arrival, through Eve's procreative potential, of the bodies—enslaved and indentured—needed to perform the vast amount of work to be done there (170–194). In *A Mercy*, Morrison has Florens read an advertisement that reveals the collapsed—indeed, seemingly non-existent—racial boundaries between and among the various forms of labor available to those with the means to purchase it:

> "A likely woman who has had small pox and measles ... A likely Negro about 9 years ... Girl or woman that is handy in the kitchen sensible, speaks good English, complexion between yellow and black ... Five years time of a white woman that understands Country work, with a child upwards of two years old ... Mulatto Fellow very much pitted with small pox, honest and sober ... White lad fit to serve ... Wanted a servant able to drive a carriage, white or black ... Sober and prudent woman who ... Likely wench, white, 29 years with child ... Healthy Deutsch woman for rent ... stout healthy, healthy strong, strong healthy likely sober ...." (*A Mercy* 52, ellipses in original)

This advertisement thus provides a snapshot of the available workforce in seventeenth-century America—a population diverse in race and gender,

but united in a class-based system of servitude. Some of the whites listed
in this advertisement—the "White lad fit to serve," for example, or the
"white woman that understands Country work, with a child upwards of
two years old" or the "Likely wench, 29, with child"—perhaps came to the
colonies aboard ships sailing from London or Bristol, the two major ports
that, David Souden observes, were the most likely points from which
indentured servants willingly (or unwillingly, in the case of those
kidnapped by unscrupulous traders) embarked for the New World. In his
study of the extant emigration registers from Bristol, Souden found a
record of indentured people very much like the individuals Morrison lists
in her fictional advertisement, and he concluded that these records
demonstrate that: "[t]he young emigrants represented here were
fundamentally part of the general degree of extra-local mobility within
pre-industrial England: they were not the rogues, the whores and the
vagabonds that the prevailing mythology might still lead us to believe"
(38).[6]

Not really "rogues" or even "vagabonds" (and certainly not "whores"),
Scully and Willard nevertheless find themselves bound into service in the
New World. Like Lina, Florens and Sorrow, they become *de facto*
members of the Vaark household, even though they are technically bound
to other property owners in the community of Milton: "For years the
neighboring farm population made up the closest either man would know
of family. A good-hearted couple (parents), and three female servants
(sisters, say) and them helpful sons" (*A Mercy* 145). Both men find Vaark
refreshingly kind as a master/employer. Willard, in particular, had
occasion to share "a tipple [of rum, a Christmas gift from Vaark] straight
from the bottle" with his social superior, and the memory of this
moment—so like the exchange of apple slices between Vaark and the
blacksmith—resonates with meaning for the indentured man. Scully and
Willard also find comfort in each other and their shared plight as
indentured servants. Soon after Scully's arrival in Milton, Morrison tells
us, a blizzard snowed in the community and the two indentured men
turned to each other for warmth as they spent the night in the barn: "There
in the warmth of animals, their own bodies clinging together, Scully
altered his plans [of running away] and Willard didn't mind at all" (*A
Mercy* 154). What is more, members of the Vaark plantation community
are not unaware of the sexual nature of the relationship between Scully
and Willard; Lina, for example, "knew he [Scully] did not object to lying
with Willard when sleep was not the point," and she recognizes that they
thus do not pose a particularly serious threat to the women on the
plantation (*A Mercy* 58).

Although they appear only briefly in course of the novel, Scully and Willard do figure importantly in the life of the community the narrative depicts. For example, it is these two men who, much to their own great delight, help Sorrow give birth to her second child. They also provide much needed male support and protection to the household following Vaark's death. Throughout *A Mercy*, then, Scully and Willard function in relation to Florens, Lina, and Sorrow much as another white indentured servant, Amy Denver, serves Sethe in *Beloved*—as a bridge between "the issues for blacks and whites" (Coonradt 182).

Further emphasizing the importance of these two men to the narrative and to the community it depicts, Morrison devotes an entire chapter, notably one of the final ones, to Scully and Willard and to their social plight. In this chapter, for instance, we learn about the restrictions on their liberty—and the challenges to their manhood—to which indentured men like Scully and Willard, despite their whiteness, were subject. The younger of the two men, Scully had, during his relatively short life, experienced a range of abuses:

> In his twenty-two years, Scully had witnessed far more human folly than Willard. By the time he was twelve he had been schooled, loved and betrayed by an Anglican curate. He had been leased to the Synod by his so-called father following his mother's death on the floor of the tavern she worked in. The barkeep claimed three years of Scully's labor to work off her indebtedness, but the "father" appeared, paid the balance due and sold his son's services, along with two casks of Spanish wine, to the Synod. (*A Mercy* 153)

Like Amy Denver in *Beloved*, Scully finds himself orphaned and then classified as legal tender to be submitted in payment for his dead mother's debts. Moreover, the system which sanctions this exchange also puts Scully into a situation in which he—like many other indentured and enslaved individuals—endures sexual and psychological abuse. The same system blames him for the abuse he suffers at the hands of one of its religious authorities, and sees to it that he is removed to "a rural area, barely populated, where, they [the Church elders] hoped, the boy might at best mend his ways or at worst have no opportunity to corrupt others" (*A Mercy* 154). From a very young age, then, Scully finds his life defined and constrained—largely without his consent—by the "legal paper" (*A Mercy* 57) on which are recorded, he faithfully believes, the terms of his indenture and the guarantee of its eventual end.

The social, legal, and personal challenges of indentured servitude also defined and constrained the trajectory of Willard's life. In presenting biographical details for Willard, who "was getting on in years and still working off his passage" (*A Mercy* 57), Morrison makes clear that his subject position as a white man was always already precarious, and—as a consequence of ever-increasing, legally imposed, and punitive lengths of service—his individual liberty was likely to be forever eluding his grasp:

> Sold for seven years to a Virginia planter, young Willard Bond expected to be freed at age twenty-one. But three years were added onto his term for infractions—theft and assault—and he was re-leased to a wheat farmer up north ... Willard overdrank and misbehaved. Early on in his post, he had run away twice, only to be caught in a tavern yard and given a further extension of his term. (*A Mercy* 149)

Reflecting further upon his lot in life, Willard notes the irony of his social position relative to a black man like the blacksmith, someone eligible for the address of "mister," when he himself is never afforded such a term of respect—except when acknowledged, possibly in jest, as "Mr. Bond" by the blacksmith himself. "Although he was still rankled by the status of a free African versus himself," Willard concludes that "there was nothing he could do about it. No law existed to defend indentured labor against them" (*A Mercy* 151).

And it is this irony of seventeenth-century racial and class politics, more so even than the complexities she brings to the characters of the blacksmith and Vaark, that is perhaps the most significant revision of the slave narrative, and the depiction of raced masculinity, introduced by Morrison in *A Mercy*. Indeed, Morrison notes that this insight, and its consequent agenda, forged her inspiration for and design of the novel:

> I was interested in separating racism from slavery. There have always been slaves, everywhere. However, only in this country are the terms so interchangeable. White people were slaves. They called themselves indentured servants. But they could be put in wills, their debts could be passed on to children, any infraction would extend their term forever. (qtd. in Bass 87)

There were, to be sure, crucial differences between white indentured servants and African slaves. Morrison states: "... they could escape, and they couldn't be found, because they were White. If you ran away as a Black person, you would be immediately recognized" (qtd. in Bass 87). As she concludes her portrait of these two white men who have, despite suffering under the burden of indenture, found a kind of love for one another and, in a very real sense, for the community of the Vaark plantation and the ideal it represents,[7] Morrison further expresses this important distinction: "Perhaps their wages were not as much as the blacksmith's, but for Scully and Mr. Bond it was enough to imagine a future" (*A Mercy* 156).

While Scully and Willard thus do not face all of the challenges of African slaves, Morrison nevertheless shows, by her generous inclusion of them in *A Mercy*, that the (neo) slave narrative and the larger conversations about power and oppression, communal and individual identity, and race and gender to which it contributes can expand to accommodate and sympathize with the complexity of these white men's stories.

-III-

Among the Library of Congress Cataloging-in-Publication Data on the copyright page of *A Mercy*, three subject areas for categorizing the novel are listed:

1. African American girls—Fiction.
2. Interracial adoption—Fiction.
3. Racism—Fiction.

While these categories certainly attend to primary concerns of the novel, they—like many of the early reviews of *A Mercy*—neglect to acknowledge the essential presence of men in the design and meaning of the narrative. As well as in her earlier book *Beloved*, it is a mistake not to recognize and interrogate Morrison's examination of white and black masculinity in her most recent work.

A consideration of what is at stake between and among men of various races and classes in the seventeenth century suggests still another shade of meaning in Morrison's cryptic title, one that looks at "a mercy" not as a noun phrase, but as an echo of the similar-sounding verb, "amerce." In the seventeenth century, the *Oxford English Dictionary* tells us, the verb "to amerce" meant, variously, "to punish" or "to deprive" (s.v., "amerce," v. 1 and 3). John Milton, for example, uses "amerce" in its latter meaning in the first book of *Paradise Lost*, where he describes Satan surveying the aftermath of his rebellion against God and its consequences for the other angels who followed him into battle:

> The fellows of his crime, the followers rather
> (Far other once beheld in bliss) condemn'd
> For ever now to have thir lot in pain,
> Millions of Spirits for his fault amerc't

Of Heav'n, and from Eternal Splendors flung
For his revolt, yet faithfull how they stood,
Thir Glory witherd. (1.606-612)[8]

Drawing on his personal experience John Hammond penned, in 1656, *Leah and Rachel, or the Two Fruitfull Sisters Virginia and Mary-Land: Their Present Condition, Impartially stated and related*, a short treatise describing life in the two colonies and detailing the best ways for individuals of various classes to avail themselves of the opportunities there. Hammond, like Milton, finds use for the verb "amerce"—this time, in its sense of "to punish"—to discuss the outcome of an uprising in Maryland, after which the losing faction met with swift colonial justice:

> Foure were presently executed . . . the rest at the importunity of some women, and resolution of some of their souldiers (who would not suffer their designe to take thorough effect, as being pricked in conscience for their ingratitudes) were saved, but were Amerced, Fined and Plundered at their pleasures. . . . (26)

Like Hammond's seventeenth-century text (and, perhaps, even Milton's) and like Morrison's earlier novel *Beloved*, *A Mercy* also speaks into being a chaotic New World community. With an early cartographic representation of that community extending, in the place of an authorial portrait, across its title-page spread, this short novel truly assumes the form of a (neo) slave narrative that realizes in particular the multiply raced and gendered subjectivities of a nation whose legacy of patriarchy, racism, classism and (hetero)sexism history will (and has)—in fiction and in reality—come both to reward and to amerce.[9]

Notes

[1] In her review of *A Mercy*, Amy Frykholm also focuses attention on Florens' narrative journey, which she considers to be "the most complex" in the novel (46). In contrast to Franklin's negative appraisal of Morrison's supposed over-emphasis on the female experience, Frykholm, however, says that, in *A Mercy*, Morrison provides "tiny glimpses into alternative ways to be human together" (47).
[2] As Carl D. Malmgren points out, many early reviewers of *Beloved* took Morrison to task for the novel's "feminist" stance, particularly regarding its sympathetic, if ultimately ambiguous, depiction of Sethe and her "crime" (101). As Nancy Kang has argued, however, there is in *Beloved* more at stake regarding masculinity than scholars have yet explored; she offers a consideration of the novel both "as a masculinist text" and as "one informed by highly misandric (or androphobic) impulses" (836). Furthermore, Dennis Childs has found in Morrison's "literary

resurrection" (272) of the American chain gang cage in *Beloved* a significant attention to the past, present and future plight of the African American male and the complex trauma of his (continuing) experience of slavery and its legacy of racial capitalism. In *Masculinist Impulses*, Nathan Grant analyzes the place of masculinity in *Beloved* as well: "Paul D's complications as a strong male figure in a text that presumably speaks principally to issues regarding black feminism interrogates some of the inner reaches of that feminism to aid in creating the discourse of a black masculinity responsive to feminism's political and social impetus" (18). More recently, Darieck Scott has also drawn attention to Paul D and to the trauma of male rape that he represents (126–171).

[3] As Cheryl Miller notes, in an otherwise unappreciative review of *A Mercy* for *Commentary*, Morrison clearly wants readers to associate her novel with Milton's epic—so much so that, as Miller has also observed, she locates the Vaark plantation in a geographic space in the New World named "Milton" (62–63). (The name of the community is mentioned in a letter that Rebekka Vaark writes for Florens to carry with her on her journey to find the blacksmith [*A Mercy* 112].) Although he does not specify the connection to Milton *per se*, John Updike also recognizes—in his equally lukewarm review of *A Mercy* for the *New Yorker*—the connection to themes of original sin, Eden, and the Fall. In her more positive review of the novel for the *Village Voice*, Leonora Todaro likewise notes the "creation myth" that figures prominently in *A Mercy*'s depiction of "the genesis of racist America."

[4] Taken in for a night by Widow Ealing, Florens observes signs of religiously motivated torture on the body of Jane, Ealing's daughter, who is under suspicion of being a demon: "I see dark blood beetling down her legs. In the light pouring over her pale skin her wounds look like live jewels" (108). Later in her stay with Ealing and Jane, Florens witnesses the continuation of this abuse: "I see Daughter Jane holding her face in her hands while the Widow freshens the leg wounds. New strips of blood gleam among the dry ones" (109). The impotency of this exorcistic ritual is ultimately made clear when Jane helps Florens get back on her way; in response to Florens' parting query about whether Jane is in fact a demon, the white girl replies, with a smile, "Yes … Oh, yes" (114).

[5] Cathy Covell Waegner has drawn attention to the grammatical peculiarity of Florens' construction "a minha mãe," with its odd combination of indefinite article and possessive (100).

[6] In *Advertisements for Runaway Slaves in Virginia, 1801–1820* and in the first volume of *Eighteenth-Century White Slaves: Fugitive Notices* (a projected four-volume series spanning the geographic range of the colonies), Daniel Meaders has compiled numerous examples of advertisements for runaway slaves and indentured servants; many demonstrate rhetoric similar to the descriptions Morrison incorporates into the notice that appears in *A Mercy*. See also Robert E. Desroches Jr.'s analysis of advertisements for the sale of slaves that appeared in Massachusetts during the eighteenth century; he finds that these notices bear witness to the fact that "New England's long history of trading slaves in print dated practically to the birth of the newspaper in colonial British America" (623). Morrison's inclusion of this document in *A Mercy* thus adds to the novel's

attention to the "mongrelization" of the colonial workforce, a situation in which, Waegner has observed, "the mongrels find themselves sifting to the bottom of social hierarchies, available for exploitation and discrimination, unsettling disturbers not comfortably fitting into the emerging white master//black slave taxonomy being put into place in the colonies" (105).

[7] After Vaark dies, Rebekka pays Scully and Willard for their labor; this change increases both their economic and their emotional connection to the community of the plantation: "The shillings she offered was the first money they had ever been paid, raising their work from duty to dedication, from pity to profit" (*A Mercy* 144).

[8] Among its examples for "amerce," the *OED* quotes line 609 of this passage from Book 1 of Milton's epic.

[9] A version of this paper was read at the 127th MLA Annual Convention in Seattle, Washington, on January 8, 2012; I would like to thank Rachael Barnett and Eden Osucha, my fellow panelists in the "More Recent Morrison" session at that meeting, for their questions and suggestions. I would also like to thank Mae Henderson and Christian Moraru for their comments on earlier versions of this essay. Any limitations of and inaccuracies in the argument remain, of course, my responsibility.

Works Cited

Bass, Patrik Henry. "Have Mercy!" Interview with Toni Morrison. *Essence.* December 2008: 87. Print.

Childs, Dennis. "'You Ain't Seen Nothin' Yet': *Beloved*, the American Chain Gang, and the Middle Passage Remix." *American Quarterly* 61 (2009): 271–297. Print.

Coonradt, Nicole M. "To Be Loved: Amy Denver and Human Need— Bridges to Understanding in Toni Morrison's *Beloved*." *College English* 32 (4) (2005): 168–187. Print.

Desrochers Jr., Robert E. "Slave-for-Sale Advertisements and Slavery in Massachusetts, 1704–1781." *The William and Mary Quarterly* 3rd ser. 59 (2002): 623–664. Print.

Franklin, Ruth. "Enslavements." Rev. of Toni Morrison's *A Mercy*. *New Republic*. December 24, 2008: 36–39. Print.

Frykholm, Amy. Rev. of Toni Morrison's *A Mercy*. *Christian Century*. February 24, 2009: 46–47. Print.

Grant, Nathan. *Masculinist Impulses: Toomer, Hurston, Black Writing, and Modernity*. Columbia: U of Missouri P, 2004. Print.

Hammond, John. *Leah and Rachel, or the Two Fruitfull Sisters Virginia and Mary-Land: Their Present Condition, Impartially stated and related*. London: Printed by T. Mabb, 1656. *Early English Books Online*. Web.

Kang, Nancy. "To Love and Be Loved: Considering Black Masculinity and the Misandric Impulse in Toni Morrison's *Beloved*." *Callaloo* 26 (2003): 836–854. Print.

Malmgren, Carl D. "Mixed Genres and the Logic of Slavery in Toni Morrison's *Beloved*." *Critique* 36 (2) (1995): 96–106. Print.

Meaders, Daniel, comp. *Advertisements for Runaway Slaves in Virginia, 1801–1820*. Studies in African American History and Culture. New York: Garland, 1997. Print.

—. *Eighteenth-Century White Slaves: Fugitive Notices, Volume 1: Pennsylvania, 1729–1760*. New York: Greenwood P, 1993. Print.

Miller, Cheryl. "Mine, Mine, Mine." Rev. of Toni Morrison's *A Mercy*. *Commentary*. March 2009: 62–64. Print.

Milton, John. *Paradise Lost*. 1674. *Complete Poems and Major Prose*. Ed. Merritt Y. Hughes. New York: Macmillan, 1957, Print.

Morrison, Toni. *Beloved*. 1987. New York: Vintage, 2004. Print.

—. *The Bluest Eye*. 1970. New York: Plume, 1994. Print.

—. *A Mercy*. New York: Knopf, 2008. Print.

—. *Playing in the Dark: Whiteness and the Literary Imagination*. New York: Vintage/Random House, 1992. Print.

Olney, James. "'I Was Born': Slave Narratives, Their Status as Autobiography and as Literature." *The Slave's Narrative*. Ed. Charles T. Davis and Henry Louis Gates, Jr. New York: Oxford UP, 1985. 225–241. Print.

Oxford English Dictionary Online.

Quilligan, Maureen. "Freedom, Service, and the Trade in Slaves: The Problem of Labour in *Paradise Lost*." *Paradise Lost: New Casebooks*. Ed. William Zunder. New York: St. Martin's, 1999. 170–194. Print.

Rice, Alan. "'Who's Eating Whom': The Discourse of Cannibalism in the Literature of the Black Atlantic from Equiano's *Travels* to Toni Morrison's *Beloved*." *Research in African Literatures* 29 (4) (1998): 107–121.

Scott, Darieck. *Extravagant Abjection: Blackness, Power, and Sexuality in the African American Literary Imagination*. New York: New York UP, 2010. Print.

Souden, David. "'Rogues, Whores and Vagabonds'? Indentured Servant Emigrants to North America and the Case of Mid-Seventeenth-Century Bristol." *Social History* 3 (1978): 23–41. Print.

Todaro, Lenora. "Toni Morrison's *A Mercy*: Racism Creation Myth." Rev. of Toni Morrison's *A Mercy*. *The Village Voice*. November 18, 2008. Web. December 20, 2011.

Updike, John. "Dreamy Wilderness." *New Yorker*. November 3, 2008: 112–113. Print.

Waegner, Cathy Covell. "Ruthless Epic Footsteps: Shoes, Migrants, and the Settlement of the Americas in Toni Morrison's *A Mercy*." *Post-national Enquiries: Essays on Ethnic and Racial Border Crossings*. Ed. Jopi Nyman. Newcastle upon Tyne, England: Cambridge Scholars Publishing, 2009, 91–112. Print.

CHAPTER THREE

BECOMING A SHE LION:
SEXUAL AGENCY IN TONI MORRISON'S
BELOVED AND *A MERCY*

ALICE EATON

This is flesh I'm talking about here. Flesh that needs to be loved. Feet that need to rest and to dance; backs that need support; shoulders that need arms, strong arms I'm telling you. And oh my people, out yonder, hear me, they do not love your neck unnoosed and straight. So love your neck; put a hand on it, grace it, stroke it, and hold it up. And all your inside parts that they'd just as soon slop for hogs, you got to love them. The dark, dark liver—love it, love it, and the beat and beating heart, love that too. More than eyes or feet. More than lungs that have yet to draw free air. More than your life-holding womb and your life-giving private parts, hear me now, love your heart. For this is the prize.

—*Beloved* 104

In her two novels of slavery, *Beloved* and *A Mercy*, Toni Morrison balances stark depictions of sexual abuse with scenes of powerful eroticism. Both novels contain an extensive catalogue of enslaved or indentured characters whose sexual lives are subject to exploitation. Despite this ever-present threat, the main character of *Beloved*, Sethe, experiences a degree of sexual agency uncommon for slave women—she conceives all four of her children with one man, of her own choosing. As a slave, Sethe is sexually abused once, an experience so traumatic it propels her to a dangerous but successful escape. Years later in the post-slavery era, her husband long gone, Sethe experiences another period of free sexual choice in her relationship with Paul D, an old friend from her slave past. In *A Mercy*, Morrison goes further in her re-envisioning of sexual agency under slavery in her creation of Florens. Florens knows she is potential prey, but escapes the deep trauma of sexual abuse. Florens' mother experiences sex only as systematic rape, but Florens herself knows only fulfilling, passionate, consensual sex. Florens, a slave, barely a woman at sixteen, and living under the repressive conditions of seventeenth-century colonial America, is paradoxically one of the most sexually free characters in all of Morrison's novels.

The trajectory from Pecola Breedlove, the main character of Morrison's first novel, *The Bluest Eye*, to Florens, by way of Sethe and other female characters in Morrison's fictional landscape, displays a distinct evolution in Morrison's thinking about sexual abuse and sexual agency for black women. In *The Bluest Eye*, Pecola has no agency, as do the other girls in the novel. In this first novel, Morrison addresses the topic of sexual abuse by drawing from the geographical area and time period in which she grew up—northern Ohio in the 1930's. Pecola falls victim to nearly everyone she meets—her mother, her teachers, her schoolmates, white shopkeepers and black neighbors—who see only "the cloak of ugliness" (*The Bluest Eye* 39) mainstream society has bestowed on her. Most tragically, of course, her father, Cholly Breedlove, rapes and impregnates her. Morrison is very deliberate in her portrayal of this final, fatal victimization in condemning not just Cholly for the act of rape, but also the forces of racism that pushed him to this desperate act. Morrison likewise condemns racism within the black community itself, as its members toss Pecola away like a piece of trash. The only advocates Pecola has are the young sisters Claudia and Frieda MacTeer, who are helpless to stop even the mean-spirited talk among the adults they hear discussing Pecola's pregnancy. All they can do is empathize with her, and for the baby inside her that everyone seems to want dead, and, of course, tell her story.

In *Sula*, Morrison explores the opposite extreme of female sexuality through her title character. Sula is never a victim; she is completely free sexually, never marrying, never becoming pregnant, sleeping with whomever she pleases. The price she pays is ostracization and isolation and, narratively speaking, an early death. It is almost as if Morrison didn't know what to do with Sula, who at age thirty "had sung all the songs there are" (*Sula* 137), and killed her off. Through Sula's character, Morrison raises important questions about the ownership of black female sexuality, and about "who was good" (146)—Sula's best friend Nel, who followed the traditional path of marriage only to face marital betrayal, or Sula, who "lived like a redwood" (142). But Sula's free sexual agency leads to a dead end. As "an artist without an art form" (121), Sula has no purpose in life. Eschewing the traditional relationships of marriage and female friendship based on loyalty and common values, she is left to her own devices and becomes bored—fatally, it seems.

Paradoxically, Morrison's most radical visions of female sexuality occur in the context of novels set during and shortly after slavery. In *Beloved* and *A Mercy*, Sethe and Florens exert a control over their sexuality that is rare in a slave culture where black women did not legally own their bodies. The prerogative of the master to have sexual relations with his female slaves was an open secret, reported powerfully in 1863 by Harriet Jacobs in her slave narrative *Incidents in the Life of a Slave Girl*. Jacobs successfully resisted her master's sexual advances, but at great cost: she violated her own moral standards by taking another white man as a lover expressly to thwart him: "I knew what I did, and I did it with deliberate calculation" (Jacobs 78). Jacobs manages to escape rape, but she did not escape years of sexual, physical and psychological harassment from her master. She lost the respect of her grandmother, who expected her (rather unrealistically)[1] to remain a virgin until she married. Jacobs' trust in the father of her two children was also violated; he ultimately married a white woman and did not make good on his promise to free her children.

Jacobs' slave narrative is groundbreaking in its frank portrayal of sexual abuse under slavery, and she is unflinching in her depiction of her abuser: "My master, to my knowledge, was the father of eleven slaves" (59). Still, Jacobs' perceived need to publish under a pseudonym and to change the names of her master and others in her story illustrates the strength of the taboo on speaking frankly about sexual abuse. Well into the twentieth century Jacobs' narrative was discredited as fiction until historian Jean Fagan Yellin authenticated it in 1981.[2] Similarly, Mary Prince, the first woman to publish a slave narrative in 1831, could only hint at sexual abuse in her story of having to bathe her master: "He had an ugly habit of stripping himself quite naked and ordering me then to wash him in a tub of water" (202). Scholars of slave narratives by women discuss "the impossibility for slave women to reveal the truth about their sexuality and sexual abuse, since abolitionist texts were designed to support the notion of a morally upright victim of the corrupt institution of slavery" (Eaton).[3]

Unconstrained by nineteenth-century mores, Morrison breaks open the taboo on speaking openly about sexuality and sexual abuse in *Beloved*. In her depiction of Sethe as a fourteen year-old girl, new to the small farm Sweet Home, taking a year to choose her husband among the male slaves on the farm, Morrison works against the "erroneous belief that [black slave women] were naturally promiscuous" (Gaspar & Hine 158). Once Sethe chooses her husband she is denied a legal wedding, but creates a wedding dress "on the sly" (*Beloved* 31). Morrison builds on research that slaves did in fact desire legal marriage, as many slave narratives attest.[4] Sethe's four children have the same father—Sethe's chosen husband, Halle—and her memory, years later, of their sexual union is sweet.[5] Sethe herself is the product of a loving union—her mother, an African slave, named her after the black man "she put her arms around" (74). Her mother's other children were the product of rape, and she is told that her mother, whom she barely knew, nevertheless "threw them all away but you" (74). Thus, Sethe learns that she is a wanted child and that children conceived in love are worth fighting for. Her mother's example establishes the foundation for her own determination to claim her own sexual, maternal and personal agency as an adult.

But Sethe does not escape sexual abuse. Six months pregnant and still nursing her youngest child, Sethe faces assault in a brutal encounter with the nephews of her new owner, Schoolteacher. The nephews, as she puts it, "took my milk" (20). Significantly, that abuse occurs in the context of her motherhood, with the cruelty focused on her nursing breasts. Several other female characters in *Beloved* experience rape that results in the birth of one or more children; among them is Ella, locked up for several years as a plaything for a father and son she dubs "the lowest yet" (301), who will not nurse the child she conceives from rape, allowing it to die; and Sethe's mother-in-law, Baby Suggs, whose eight children are fathered by six different men, several of whom trick her into sex with false promises to protect her children. For Sethe, the assault on her breasts is as serious a violation as vaginal rape and pushes her to escape from Sweet Home. The men severely beat her after she reports the assault to her helpless mistress, but it is the sexual assault that outrages her, not the beating. Paul D asks her:

"They used cowhide on you?"
"And they took my milk!"
"They beat you and you was pregnant?"
"And they took my milk!" (20)

Sethe's desperate act of resistance when Schoolteacher comes for her and her children after her escape to Ohio is a salient moment in the narrative—her successful killing of one child and attempt to kill all four. This aspect of Sethe's story is based in the historical facts of the fugitive slave Margaret Garner's life.[6] Other than the assault on Sethe's breasts, Morrison's depiction of her main character's sexual agency is remarkably unpoliced within the context of slavery. Sethe's involvement in a degraded sexual encounter occurs again when she pays for the tombstone engraving for her murdered child by having sex with the engraver. Numbed by the loss of her child, she nevertheless exerts choice in this encounter, not anticipating how it would linger in her consciousness for years to come. She reflects later that: "I got close … [t]o being a Saturday girl" (241). The character Sethe represents her avoidance of a life of prostitution as almost by chance; the author, however, makes a deliberate choice to depict Sethe as a woman with agency in her sexual life.

In the post-slavery era, after years of being alone, Sethe again enters into a loving, satisfying sexual relationship with Paul D, a former slave she had known at Sweet Home. Morrison's description of their initial sexual encounter recalls both characters' memories of Sethe's first sexual experience with Halle in a cornfield, which Paul D witnesses from a nearby hill, the corn stalks dancing in the sun. The corn scene is one of the most erotic passages in all of Morrison's writing:

> She remembered that some of the corn stalks broke, folded down over Halle's back, and among the things her fingers clutched were husk and cornsilk hair.
> How loose the silk. How jailed down the juice.
> The jealous admiration of the watching men melted with the feast of new corn they allowed themselves that night … Paul D couldn't remember how they'd finally cooked those ears too young to eat. What he did remember was the parting of the hair to get to the tip, the edge of his fingernail just under, so as not to graze a single kernel.
> The pulling down of the tight sheath, the ripping sound always convinced her it hurt.
> As soon as one strip of husk was down, the rest obeyed and the ear yielded up to him its shy rows, exposed at last. How loose the silk. How quick the jailed-up flavor ran free.
> No matter what all your teeth and wet fingers anticipated, there was no accounting for the way that simple joy could shake you.
> How loose the silk. How fine and loose and free. (32-3)

This passage appears in the second chapter of the novel. Though the action occurs in the post-emancipation era, nearly twenty years after Sethe's harrowing escape from slavery, the scene signals early on that Sethe is a woman able to exert control over her sexuality.

Sethe goes through a crucible over the course of the novel, as her dead child comes back to haunt and torture her. But unlike Sula, Morrison allows the character to live, and the author provides hope that Sethe will survive and perhaps even thrive, with the love and help of her lover Paul D. When a community of women finally exorcise the ghost-child, and Sethe lies in bed broken and hopeless, Paul D comes to her bedside. She speaks of her murdered child: "She was my best thing" (321).

"Sethe," [Paul D] says, "me and you, we got more yesterday than anybody.
We need some kind of tomorrow."
He leans over and takes her hand. With the other he touches her face. "You
your best thing, Sethe. You are." His holding fingers are holding hers.
"Me? Me?" (322)

Though the power of her inescapable "rememories" has beaten Sethe
down, this final vision of her character indicates that she may be able to
move on, now that she has faced her traumatic past. She claims agency
over herself with the words "Me? Me?", but the question marks leave her
future and her ability to heal uncertain, if hoped for, for the reader.

In *A Mercy*, Morrison goes even further in her exploration of sexual
agency for black women under slavery. Unlike *Beloved*, in which Morrison
depicts a character who experiences both sexual abuse *and* sexual
freedom, *A Mercy* centers on a character nearly untouched by sexual
abuse. Though *A Mercy* is set in the earliest historical period of all
Morrison's novels, it is also a product of the early Twenty-First Century in
its radical re-envisioning of black female sexuality. Just as *Sula* was a
response to the second wave of the women's movement in the late 1960s
and early 1970s, *A Mercy* reflects the world of its publication year, 2008,
when black women of the Obama family were preparing to move into the
White House as members of the First Family of the United States.

In *A Mercy*, Morrison separates her depiction of sexual abuse from
sexual agency by locating these concepts in separate characters. Readers
learn early in the novel that Florens' mother, referred to only as minha-
mãe, Portuguese for "my mother," is likely the sexual object of her owner,
D'Ortega. Florens' mother's presence looms large throughout the novel, as
Florens recalls what to her was an abandonment, when her mother allowed
her to be payment for D'Ortega's debt to Jacob Vaark, a Northern trader.
Florens' first- person narration is interspersed with chapters in the third
person focused on other characters, and Florens' voice provides a
powerful through line for the story. Morrison discusses her creation of
Florens' narrative voice, asserting that she was not interested in creating
an accurate depiction of someone moving from Portuguese to English, as
Florens did: "Instead of trying to do what they call a 'language of the
period,' or some dialect that I couldn't even invent, I found her voice by
simply making sure she only spoke in the present tense" ("An Evening
with Toni Morrison," Lisner Auditorium). Despite this assertion, Morrison
employs a great deal of inventiveness in the creation of Florens' voice, in
her proliferation of action verbs in place of adjectives, in passages such as
"And when I see you and fall into you I know I am live" (136)—not alive,
but live; and "I am shock" (121)—not shocked, but shock. Stylistically,

the novel is Faulknerian with its shifting narrative voices and sometimes opaque prose, but it is also rooted firmly in the twenty-first century, particularly because of the narrative voice of Florens, a literate, confident, sexually free black woman, who is paradoxically a slave.

But the slavery Florens experiences is not typical, in part because of the family that owns her, and also because slavery has not yet gone through the "Terrible Transformation" which "irrevocably linked servitude to skin color" (Tally 63). In 1690, when the novel is set, ideas about slavery are more fluid, particularly in the north where Florens lives with the Vaarks. In "Mary's Land," where she was born and where her mother and brother still live, plantation slavery was well on its way to the racial stratification and systematic abuse that became its hallmark. For this very reason, Florens' mother instinctively senses that the northerner, Jacob Vaark, will not treat Florens the way she herself has been treated. The mother's chapter which ends *A Mercy* departs from the established structure of the novel; the minha-mãe is the only other character besides Florens to speak in the first- person. The power of this short chapter at the end of the novel cannot be overstated; readers finally learn directly from the minha-mãe why she urges Vaark to take Florens. It was not an abandonment, but "a mercy"; the minha-mãe trusted Vaark to make sure Florens did not experience what she did on D'Ortega's plantation, where "to be a female in this place is to be an open wound that cannot heal" (163), and her judgment that Vaark would not abuse Florens is correct.

Florens senses only dimly the traumas she has escaped when a man's hand brushes her backside as she enters a carriage. She knows enough to be careful of drunken men during a portion of the novel when she is traveling alone, but she learned this from her surrogate mother, Lina, a Native American servant in the Vaark household, who "had fallen in love" (70) with Florens as soon as Jacob brought her home. Lina's love is not enough to keep Florens from her heart-stopping desire for the blacksmith, a free black man who comes to work for Vaark. Florens is heedless of Lina's warnings against the blacksmith, but it is not exploitation Lina worries about, it is desire, and Florens' desire is overpowering.

A scene of Florens' lovemaking with the blacksmith provides another of Morrison's supremely rendered erotic descriptions. Sorrow, another servant in the Vaark household, witnesses the lovers. Sorrow's sexual history consists solely of rape, and she watches in wonder:

> The blacksmith and Florens were rocking and, unlike female farm animals in heat, she was not standing quietly under the weight and thrust of the male. What Sorrow saw yonder in the grass under a hickory tree was not the silent submission to the slow goings behind a pile of wood or a hurried

one in a church pew that Sorrow knew. This here female stretched, kicked her heels and whipped her head left, right, to, fro. It was a dancing. Florens rolled and twisted from her back to his. He hoisted her up against the hickory; she bent her head into his shoulder. A dancing. (151)

The blacksmith is an almost mythical figure of pure desire. He is never named, and his status as a free man makes him untouchable. Vaark treats him as an equal, and he, in turn, treats the white male indentured servants who work for Vaark as equals, who fall under the spell of his boundless charisma and easy charm. Morrison never allows readers access to the blacksmith's point of view, so his character functions primarily as an idealized figure of desire and freedom. Nevertheless, the blacksmith provides Florens with a valuable lesson, if she is capable of learning it. When their love affair is irrevocably severed, largely due to Florens' inability to free herself from her overwhelming desire for him, he tells her she is: "a slave by choice ... nothing but wilderness. No constraint. No mind" (166–7). He tells her: "Own yourself, woman" (166).

The blacksmith refers to Florens as "wilderness" in response to her violent behavior. He leaves her to care for a young boy, Malaik, for several days. Out of jealousy that the boy is stealing the blacksmith's attention, Florens grabs Malaik roughly, accidentally injuring him. When the blacksmith orders her to leave, she goes wild, attacking him with a hammer and tongs from the fireplace. Her behavior is shocking, particularly since she minimizes it: "I do hear the shoulder crack but the sound is small," and "Yes, there is blood. A little" (164–5). But by the end of her narration, Florens accepts her wildness as an integral part of herself, with the implication that she will use it more wisely, and not allow herself to be overpowered by the forces of desire that drove her to worship the blacksmith.

Florens' first-person narration has been directed to the blacksmith throughout the novel, and in her last section of narration, readers discover that she has been writing her words down. She writes not on paper, but on the floors and walls of the opulent, unfinished and never-to-be-occupied house Jacob Vaark builds before his early death. Symbolically, Florens' writing of her story can be seen as a "dismantling of the master's house," to borrow Audre Lorde's famous words, and as if obeying Lorde's instructions, Florens creates her own "tools"—she does not use the "master's tools to dismantle the master's house" (Lorde 110). Florens uses her own unique voice as a dismantling tool, as she writes her story to the blacksmith.

With deep irony, Florens remembers at the end of her writing that the blacksmith does not know how to read. This realization frees her from her need for him, and she resolves to burn down the house in order to release her words "to the air that is out in the world ... to fly up then fall, fall like ash over acres of primrose and mallow" where they will finally "flavor the soil of the earth" (188). Releasing her words to the air and the earth, she moves beyond mere sexual agency in her freedom to welcome a lover of her choice, to a full-fledged agency of self, as she declares: "I am become wilderness, but I am also Florens. In full. Unforgiven. Unforgiving ... Slave. Free. I last" (189).

The contrast between Florens and the protagonist of Morrison's first novel, Pecola Breedlove, displays a remarkable progression from girl victim to a young woman in full command of herself. Florens is an agent in her own life, and her status as a slave is nearly irrelevant. Florens lives the notion of freedom as set out in Frederick Douglass' famous slave narrative, *Narrative of the Life of Frederick Douglass*—she may be a slave "in form" but not "in fact."[7] Late in the novel, after she understands that the blacksmith will never forgive her, Florens still recalls his lesson about freedom: "You say you see slaves freer than free men" (187). The blacksmith's words here are a clear echo of Douglass' perception of the possibility of mental freedom for enslaved people. Morrison evokes the image of a lion, often associated with Douglass,[8] in the blacksmith's description of slaves and free men: "One is a lion in the skin of an ass. The other is an ass in the skin of a lion" (187). However, she suggests that this vision of a slave as a secret "lion" does not encompass the female slave experience, as Florens builds on the blacksmith's lesson to create her own identity: "Still, there is another thing. A lion who thinks his mane is all. A she-lion who does not" (187–8).

In addition to evoking images of Frederick Douglass, Morrison's focus on the male lion's mane can be interpreted as a comment on the complications of gender and freedom for slaves. Florens differentiates herself from the slave as male lion in disguise. She implies that the mane is one more thing to hide behind, but as a female, she has no mane. As a female slave or "she-lion," she is even more exposed than a male slave who has asserted himself as a slave "in form," if no longer "in fact." Harriet Jacobs asserts, "Slavery is terrible for men; but it is far more terrible for women" (101), and claiming one's freedom under slavery is far riskier for female slaves. Yet Florens takes that risk: "Slave. Free. I last" (189).

Morrison has said, contrary to what many say about her work, that she believes her novels end happily because her characters learn something.[9] The contrast between the ending of *The Bluest Eye*, which affirms that it is "much, much, much too late" (206) to save Pecola, with the ending of *A*

Mercy, which allows the readers hope that Florens has learned and will thrive, illustrates a progressively more radical vision of black female sexuality in Morrison's later work.[10] Crucial to the possibility of Florens' hopeful future is the support and intervention of mother figures in her life: her minha-măe, who reveals to readers in the last chapter that Florens has been spared a life of rape and abuse as a plantation slave; Lina, who raised Florens after her arrival at the Vaarks', and with whom Florens plots a burning of Jacob's useless mansion; and Sorrow, the witness to Florens' sexual passion and agency, who changes her name and plans escape from the Vaark household, urging Florens to join her.

Thus, *A Mercy* is anything but a prequel to Morrison's earlier novel of slavery, *Beloved*. In *Beloved*, Morrison provides a female protagonist who, despite the deep traumas of her slave experience, is able to rise above her sexual, physical and psychological abuse and claim her own agency as a sexual being, a mother and, finally, as a free person. Morrison also signals a progressive vision of black female sexuality in *Beloved* through the character of Baby Suggs, whose own history of rape under slavery does not prohibit her from urging her granddaughter Denver "to listen to [your] body and love it," in defiance of the idea that "Slaves [are] not supposed to have pleasurable feelings on their own" (*Beloved* 247). In *A Mercy*, Morrison's vision is even more progressive in her creation of Florens, who is relatively unscathed by slavery. The loss of her minha-măe when she was a child was certainly traumatic but saves her from much worse. Florens' worst trauma as an adult is a broken heart, which forces her to claim herself as a "she-lion" of self-determination. Florens' ability to exert sexual agency in her choice of lover is a crucial step in her process of becoming this "she-lion," a slave woman "freer than free men" (*A Mercy* 187), freer than Morrison's earlier protagonist Sula, whose freedom is cut short by early death.

Though Florens will never explicitly know the "mercy" her mother provided her by sending her away from the plantation, she reflects with satisfaction that she has achieved something her mother wished for her. Her mother's early concerns for her daughter and her "prettify ways" are symbolized by Florens' insistence on wearing shoes, which will give her the impractical "feet of a Portuguese lady," "too tender for life" and the toughness "that life requires" (4). At the end of her final section of narration, Florens explains to her mother, despite knowing she cannot hear her, that her feet, and by extension her adult self, have been toughened as a result of her long, barefoot journey away from the blacksmith: "Măe, you can have pleasure now because my feet are hard as cypress" (189).

Even if critics disagree about whether Florens is irrevocably damaged or empowered at the end of the novel, there is no denying the power of the eroticism in her sexual union with the blacksmith. I argue that because Florens has only known choice in her sexual life, and her claim of herself at the end of the novel provides hope for the reader that she will survive, even in a world where the odds are stacked against her due to her race and gender. She may escape from slavery altogether by running away with Sorrow, who is also empowered by her witnessing of Florens' sexual ecstasy, showing Sorrow that sex does not consist of only of rape. Even if Florens remains a slave, as Rebekkah's property or sold to someone else, she has claimed her sense of agency. At the end of the novel, she is a slave in form, but not in fact.

The final chapter of the novel, written in the minha-mãe's voice, likewise addresses the daughter who cannot hear:

> It was not a miracle. Bestowed by God. It was a mercy. Offered by a human. I stayed on my knees. In the dust where my heart will remain each night and every day until you understand what I know and long to tell you: to be given dominion over another is a hard thing; to wrest dominion over another is a wrong thing; to give dominion of yourself to another is a wicked thing. (196)

These final words, which Florens does not hear, nevertheless provide hope for readers, because it is clear that Florens has already learned her mother's lesson on her own. She has become a "she-lion," a grown woman, with dominion over herself.

Notes

[1] Jacobs' grandmother, a mother of five children, was possibly an object of sexual abuse herself. Jacobs never mentions who fathered her grandmother's children, though she does emphasize that she and her brother were conceived in a marriage of choice between their two slave parents. In addition, Jacobs credits her mother's status as a mulatto to "the complexion my grandmother had derived from Anglo-Saxon ancestors" (31), not from her unidentified grandfather. Also, a vexed question for scholars of Jacobs' life and work is whether she is concealing the fact that she *was* actually raped by her master, a much more likely scenario than the one she paints of resistance. See Jennifer Fleischner's (2010) introduction to *Incidents*.

[2] Henry Louis Gates, Jr. writes of Yellin's efforts to legitimize Jacobs' narrative that "Few instances of scholarly inquiry have been more important to Afro-American studies than Yellin's" (xvii).

[3] See Moira Ferguson's 1998 introduction to Prince's narrative and Alice Knox Eaton's article on Prince in the African American National Biography. Patricia Morton's *Discovering the Women in Slavery* provides a more general discussion of the constraints on female slaves and ex-slaves in revealing sexual abuse.

[4] The 1856 collection, *A North-Side View of Slavery*, compiled by Benjamin Drew, contains dozens of slave narratives of fugitive slaves in Canada, mostly stories of men. A recurring theme of these short narratives is the longing for wives and children left behind in bondage. One slave narrator, Dan Josiah Lockhart, asserts: "The hardest thing in slavery is not the work,--it is the abuse of a man, and in my case, of a man's wife and children. They were not punished severely,--but I did not want her whipped at all—I don't want any man to meddle with my wife,--I bothered her enough, and didn't want anybody else to trouble her at all" (49). Lockhart expresses in these not so veiled words his fear that his wife will be raped while in slavery.

[5] Margaret Garner, the slave woman on whom Sethe's character is based, was not so lucky. Margaret had a slave husband, Robert Garner, who lived on a neighboring farm, and with whom she had her first child. Her younger children were light-skinned and almost certainly the product of rape. In 2005, the opera "Margaret Garner," for which Morrison wrote the libretto, opened in Cincinnati, and a tour was arranged for cast members of the farm where Garner was enslaved by Archibald K. Gaines. On the tour, a Gaines family representative asserted that the relationship between their ancestor and his slave Margaret was consensual, setting off a heated confrontation with cast members including Denyce Graves, who portrayed Garner. See Gelfand, "Hot Debate over Escape from Slavery."

[6] Margaret Garner's life is discussed in a variety of sources. I have listed two on my Works Cited page: a brief encyclopedic entry by Quintard Taylor and an article by Angelita Reyes.

[7] After successfully defying his master, Douglass writes: "I now resolved that, however long I might remain a slave in form, the day had passed forever when I could be a slave in fact" (89).

[8] Douglass is referred to as a lion in many different sources. I have noted one, *The Colored Orator* by Frederic May Holland, on my Works Cited page.

[9] Morrison answered a question about the endings of her novels at a talk at Oberlin College on March 14, 2012, saying her books have "happy endings because at the end the character has learned, acquired knowledge, so that's happy."

[10] In Morrison's newest novel, *Home*, she includes a depiction of a black woman sexually victimized, this time by the medical establishment, in her story of Cee abused by her doctor/employer in a medical experiment that leaves her unable to bear children. Cee's story is important to the narrative, but she is not the main character; the novel focuses primarily on her brother Frank and his struggles as an African American man and a Korean War veteran in the 1950s. Morrison's authorial impulse to return to the issue of sexual abuse, and the weakest victims of it, like Pecola and Cee, is strong. Equally strong is her counterbalancing impulse to portray potent visions of eroticism where her female characters are strongly fulfilled. If there is a pattern in Morrison's work, perhaps readers can expect a

powerful scene of eroticism in her next novel after focusing mostly on sexual abuse in *Home*.

Works Cited

Douglass, Frederick. *Narrative of the Life of Frederick Douglass*. Ed. David W. Blight. Boston: Bedford/St. Martin's, 2003.

Drew, Benjamin, ed. *A North-Side View of Slavery*. Boston: John P. Jewett and Company, 1856. Documenting the American South. University of North Carolina at Chapel Hill. May 22, 2012. http://docsouth.unc.edu/neh/drew/drew.html

Eaton, Alice Knox. "Prince, Mary." *African American National Biography*, eds. Henry Louis Gates, Jr. and Evelyn Brooks Higginbotham. Oxford: Oxford University Press, 2008.

Ferguson, Moira (ed). *The History of Mary Prince*. Ann Arbor: University of Michigan Press, 1998.

Gaspar , David Barry & Darlene Clark Hine (eds.). *More Than Chattel: Black Women and Slavery in the Americas*. Bloomington: Indiana University Press, 1996.

Gates, Henry Louis, Jr. (ed.). *The Classic Slave Narratives*, New York: Penguin, 1987.

Gelfand, Janelle. "Hot Debate over Escape from Slavery." Cincinnati.com. July 10, 2005. Web. May 22, 2012. http://news.cincinnati.com/article/20050710/ENT07/507100324/Hot-Debate-over-escape-from-slavery

Jacobs, Harriet. *Incidents in the Life of a Slave Girl*. Ed. Jennifer Fleischner. Boston: Bedford/St. Martin's, 2010.

Holland, Frederic May. *Frederick Douglass: The Colored Orator*. New York: Funk & Wagnall's, 1895. Documenting the American South. University of North Carolina at Chapel Hill. May 22, 2012. http://docsouth.unc.edu/neh/holland/holland.html

Lorde, Audre. "The Master's Tools Will Never Dismantle the Master's House." In *Sister Outsider*. Berkeley: Crossing Press, 1984.

Morrison, Toni. *Beloved*. New York: Random House, 2004.

—. *The Bluest Eye*. New York: Penguin, 1994.

—. "An Evening with Toni Morrison." Lisner Auditorium, George Washington University, Washington, D. C. September 21, 2011. Web. May 22, 2012. http://www.youtube.com/watch?v=ocVG7W4HxvM

—. "An Evening with Toni Morrison." Finney Chapel, Oberlin College, Oberlin, Ohio. March 14, 2012.

—. *A Mercy*. New York: Random House, 2009.

—. *Sula*. New York: Random House, 2004.

Morton, Patricia (ed.). *Discovering the Women in Slavery: Emancipating Perspectives on the American Past*. Athens: University of Georgia Press, 1996.

Prince, Mary. *The History of Mary Prince*. In *The Classic Slave Narratives* (ed.). Henry Louis Gates, Jr. New York: Penguin, 1987.

Reyes, Angelita. "Using History as Artifact to Situate *Beloved*'s Unknown Woman: Margaret Garner." In *Approaches to Teaching the Novels of Toni Morrison*, eds. Nellie Y. McKay and Kathryn Earle. New York: Modern Language Association, 1997.

Tally, Justine. "Contextualizing Toni Morrison's Ninth Novel: What Mercy? Why Now?" In *Toni Morrison's A Mercy: Critical Contexts*, eds. Shirley A. Stave and Justine Tally. Newcastle Upon Tyne: Cambridge Scholars Press, 2011.

Taylor, Quintard. *Margaret Garner Incident (1856)*. Blackpast.org. Web. May 22, 2012.
http://www.blackpast.org/?q=aah/margaret-garner-incident-1856

CHAPTER FOUR

THE NATURAL AND LEGAL GEOGRAPHIES OF THE BODY: LAW'S CORPUS WRITTEN ON THE LIVES OF FLORENS AND SETHE

KATHRYN MUDGETT

Under the pines of Sweet Home, Mister the rooster, enthroned on a tub, holds dominion over the hens and stares at Paul D walking by with a bit in his mouth. Paul D later swears to Sethe that Mister had smiled at him, a slave who was "something less than a chicken sitting in the sun on a tub" (*Beloved* 86). Sweet Home, where Sethe herself has seen "boys hanging from the most beautiful sycamores in the world," is the slaves' Kentucky domicile by operation of law that designates their master Garner's home as their own. What Sethe and Paul D have not been able to choose by intent, the law has designated for them: "Mister [is] allowed to be and stay what he [is]," but Paul D and Sethe are assigned their place by law and without their will (85). Sweet Home, the antithesis of domestic tranquility under Schoolteacher's rule, is the tangible manifestation of the authoritative voice of the law that has reduced its slaves' condition to less than a barnyard animal. Sweet Home's fields and buildings were not planted or constructed alone by unfree hands, but by the law that bound them.

Toni Morrison's body of work is a response to this decreative force of the law on the life of the slave, as she seeks to "insert [her] imagination and African-Americans into that history" of the New World whose corpus of law would be inscribed on the body of the slave, causing all of the slave's descendants to suffer the consequences of the man-made division between her natural and legal body (Toomer 21). By a legal fiction, the slave in early America was diminished from personhood to a legally constructed admixture of property and person, a deconstruction of the individual by construction of law. Morrison's response to this decreative legal force is the creative power of literature to reclaim the natural identity and humanity of the slave through the slave's own narrative voice. Morrison has noted that while there has been "no civilization that did not rest on some form of enslavement," the racial basis of slavery sprang *sui generis* from the ostensibly Edenic New World (Morrison, "Interview"). In the seventeenth-century colonial world of landed gentry, indentured servants, free blacks and slaves recreated in *A Mercy*, race-based slavery, in Morrison's words, "had to be constructed, planted, institutionalized, and legalized" ("Interview"). Morrison saw this historical setting, where racial laws had only begun to arise ad hoc, as her literary opportunity to "separate race from slavery," "to see what it might have been like to be a slave without being raced" ("Interview").

A Mercy (2008), set in seventeenth-century Mary's Land, precedes the post-Civil War Ohio setting of *Beloved* (1987) historically, but follows in Morrison's canon and represents a staggering expansion of her examination of what she has called the "house/home antagonism," in which "the body as consummate home" is "estranged ... legislated ... violated, rejected, [and] deprived" of its self-identity and sovereignty ("Home" 5). Because the world of *A Mercy* is as yet the New World, Morrison can address its fall from Edenic grace as whiteness constructed first through custom and then through law, to subordinate and exclude all those deemed "other." Through the interactions of servants, slaves, Native Americans and masters, Morrison manages a consummate achievement— the narrative exposition of the reification of whiteness as the sole objective manifestation of personhood in the land. Reification is defined as the "mental conversion of an abstract concept into a material thing" (*Black's Law Dictionary* 1312; hereafter *BLD*), and this process of establishing white privilege over time in the New World and new nation as a valorized property interest also established whiteness as a "an aspect of self-identity and personhood," characterized by a right to exclude (Harris 1725, 1735.)

What Morrison has termed "this little perk called whiteness"—used to divide the poor from each other and from those who make the laws—has only begun to taint the Vaark farm of *A Mercy*, where Florens, Messalina (Lina), Sorrow, Rebekka, and the indentured servants Willard and Scully form "a little society ... in the wilderness," what is for Morrison "the earliest version of American individuality and self-sufficiency" (Morrison, "Interview"). Over the ensuing years this promise is bedeviled through legal construction, and by the time of the nation's founding a century later those whose labor is owned are both raced and "debased by servitude below the equal level of free inhabitants; which regards the *slave* as divested of two fifths of the *man*" (*Federalist* No. 54; emphases in original).

In Morrison's work, *A Mercy* portrays a New World as neither prelapsarian nor dark and destructive as the postlapsarian world in which *Beloved*'s Sethe makes her choice. *A Mercy* is but the beginning of the process of decreating the black slave, of separating her from indentured servants whose labor is owned by others but whose humanity is not compromised by law. In *Beloved*, the decreation is a fait accompli. Morrison's recreation of the interior life of the slave, through the voices of Florens and Sethe, reintegrates the slave's body into an identifiable human being, despite her being orphaned from civilization by law.

In *A Mercy*, custom precedes the codification of law that valorizes whiteness in the transformation from selfhood to servitude for all others.[1] It is a measure of Morrison's achievement in *A Mercy* that the people of Vaark's farm embody the as-yet-unborn nation's process of construction of whiteness as both identity and valued property interest, tracing a pattern of exclusion first perpetuated by habit and then enshrined in law. This process of depersonalization is most fully revealed in *A Mercy* through Florens' story.

The law is the instrumentality by which the slave's humanity is compromised by codification, inscribed in books to which the unlettered slave has no access. In seventeenth-century Mary's Land, Florens' mother determines that "learning" is imperative to survival and has Reverend Father teach the child to read and write. "Very quickly I can write from memory the Nicene Creed including all the commas," boasts Florens, the slave child, of the fruits of her lessons from Reverend Father, who is forbidden by law to teach her (*A Mercy* 6). A proudly lettered slave, Florens explicitly refers to only three writings in the course of her story: a profession of faith in God, recited with the promise of "happiness when this life is done" (6); a letter of passage required by law, proving Florens is "nobody's minion" but her owner's (111); and Florens' own history carved with a nail into the floor and walls of her dead master's house, a monument to his excess built with the profits of Barbadian slave labor. These texts define her life as chattel, as a woman smitten by both God's and man's law, where "nothing in the catechism" taught by the priest can protect her from a lifetime of servitude codified by statute (163).

Both Florens and her mother are baptized in "Mary's Land," before Florens is taken north by Jacob Vaark in payment for Senor D'Ortega's debt. Neither mother nor child has any expectation of protection in this life by her recital of faith—Florens looks toward an afterlife for possible happiness, and her minha mãe, a survivor of the Barbadian cane fields, "trie[s] to tell Reverend Father" of her doubt in the protective or consolatory power of God's love (*A Mercy* 164). Minha mãe believes only in the power of "learning" and holds the hope that if her daughter "learn[s] letters" she may "somehow someday ... make [her] way" (163). The colonial law of Maryland, where mother and daughter profess their faith, excludes them, though Christianized, from recognition as free inhabitants of the province. As early as 1639, "An Act for the Liberties of the People" provided that "all the Inhabitants of this Province being Christians (Slaves excepted) Shall have and enjoy all such rights, liberties, immunities, priviledges, and free customs within this Province as any naturall born subject of England ..." (1 *Md. Arch.* 41 [1639]). While invoking the law of England to protect "the liberties of the people," the language of the Maryland act reserved the right to alter or change the mother country's law, to ensure the province's right, in Jacob Vaark's words, to "separate[ ] and protect[ ] all whites from all others forever" (*A Mercy* 10).

Even as the "Europes" took flight from the Old World to the New, they sought to establish a distinction between themselves and, as Morrison has written: "the presence of the unfree within the heart of the democratic experiment" (*Playing in the Dark* 48). To Morrison, others' enslavement "highlighted freedom—if it did not in fact create it—" for those who would come to embody the "quintessential American identity"—"new, white, and male" (43, 44). In *A Mercy*, Morrison's characters indict both human and natural law espoused by the "Europes" to assert dominion over "lesser people" (99). The young slave Florens accepted in payment for a debt, the Native American slave Lina supposedly Christianized but embracing her heathen-ness, and the bereft slave Sorrow who lost a child and possibly her mind all struggle in a world where "lawless laws" deny their humanity (10). The indentured servants Willard and Scully, even though "Europes," suffer the indignities of servitude to masters who invent crimes against them or lease them to others to extend their terms, while chafing at the freedoms enjoyed by the black smithy working on Vaark's monumental house with them. Even Rebekka Vaark, wife of the slaves' owner, has been bought and brought from the Old World to "this fresh and new England" to wed and serve her master (90). In the colonial world represented by Morrison's characters, "[u]nfreedom [is] not an aberration: freedom [is]" (Wiecek 1792).

From early colonial times, however, as William Wiecek has written, African Americans' "unfreedom was different in kind from the control imposed" on other "not-Europes"—the freedmen, Native Americans, and indentured servants who also lived a benighted existence among the free (Wiecek 1781). A cogent example is the succession of Maryland laws passed to ensure no slave such as Florens or her mother could gain freedom by baptism. Having excepted Christian slaves from the enjoyment of the liberties of the people in 1639, the Maryland proprietors remained vigilant about the danger of slaves "p'tending to be Christned And soe pleade the lawe of England" (1 *Md. Arch.* 526 [1664]), where by common law dating back to the early 1600s a slave who was baptized became free (Catterall I: 55). To avoid any confusion about a slave's status within the province, the Maryland Assembly passed an act in 1664 "obligeing negros to serve durante vita," extending servitude for life regardless of religious condition (1 *Md. Arch.* 526 [1664]). When that law failed to dispel the mistaken belief that "by becomeing Christians [slaves] and the Issues of their bodies are actually manumited and made free and discharged from their Servitude and bondage," the Maryland Assembly explicitly provided in 1671 that no "negro slave" baptized or Christianized before or after importation into the province was thereby free (2 *Md. Arch.* 272 [1671]).

Mary's Land displaces divine law and its principles of moral right and wrong with the positive law of man, ordering "human activities and relations through the systematic application of the force of politically organized society" within a purportedly Christian community (*BLD* 900). God's law is trumped by restrictive laws against black "not-Europes" "established by human authority" and designed to prevent the emancipation of those deemed unworthy of the liberties of free people (*BLD* 1200). Florens' recital of the Nicene Creed cannot inject her into the moral sphere of Christian faith; she can still be valued at "twenty pieces of eight" in payment for a debt and sent north with a stranger (*A Mercy* 27).

The notion of a "*law* of slavery" is paradoxical in its acknowledgement of a body of law that is "inherently lawless, illegitimate, and unjust" (Wiecek 1773). If justice requires fair administration of the laws, then laws in direct conflict with moral principles would beg the question of legitimacy and preclude fair application. Some few free and enslaved people acknowledge this contradiction openly in *A Mercy*: Jacob Vaark ruminates on the "lawless laws" of the territory he passes through to collect a debt (10); Florens' mother says "Unreason rules here" of life under a legalized system of physical abuse by lash (164). Lina, the Native American slave owned by Vaark, has no delusions about the purported Christianity of the "Europes" who both declare their faith and enforce human law directly opposed to natural law. Lina is described in an advertisement for her sale as a "[h]ardy female, Christianized and capable in all matters domestic available for exchange of goods or specie," but her "faith" is a product of her fear of abandonment by those who rescued her from her native village when it was burned by "Europes" to prevent the spread of sickness (*A Mercy* 52). She rejects the religious teachings of the Presbyterians, who assign her people's destruction by disease to "God's wrath" at the "idle and profane"; who never ask her about the healed lash marks covering her body; and who sell her to Jacob Vaark when her conversion proves a failure (47, 48). Lina understands that she has no legitimacy in human society: "no standing in law, no surname and no one [to] take her word against a Europe" if she were to protest her treatment (52). "Purchased outright and deliberately" by Vaark, Lina, whose given name even she does not know, is subject to her master's authority and dependent on his very existence (34). If Vaark dies and his widow follows him, Lina, like Florens, like Sorrow and her newborn child, will be merely "illegal," "subject to purchase, hire, assault, abduction, exile" (58).

Vaark prides himself on his collection of women, all of whom he believes he has rescued rather than acquired through purely commercial transactions to procure reliable help for his farm (34). Carefully distinguishing his human acquisitions as rescues, Vaark can convince himself that he has saved each one from "whips, chains and armed overseers" even as he holds them in perpetual servitude (28). The "dregs" of Vaark's Protestantism allow him the pretense of moral superiority over wealthy landowners "dependent on a captured workforce" maintained by violence, deluding himself that men such as D'Ortega have "trad[ed their] conscience for coin" while Vaark remains morally blameless (28). Vaark, so seemingly attuned to the plight of homeless "waifs ... whelps" and the "ill-shod child [Florens] that the mother was throwing away" has, like other nominal Christians, orphaned his own moral compass for the sake of secular wealth (32, 34).

Vaark's death is his final selfish act of "dominion" over the women in his household, leaving a wife but no other legitimate heir (*A Mercy* 167). With his widow Rebekka's life in the balance, Lina, Sorrow and Florens are destined to be "interlopers, squatters" should she die (58). Ironically, as Florens goes in search of the free black smithy who will cure her mistress's disease, her only protection is the law that dehumanizes her, in the form of a letter signed by her mistress validating her travel. Florens understands the power of the written word to both enslave and protect her. Rebekka Vaark's letter asserts that Florens is "owned by me and can be knowne by a burne mark in the palm of her left hand. Allow her the courtesie of safe passage ...." (112). The letter has the force of law granted by Rebekka's words: It proves, says Florens, that "I am nobody's minion but my Mistress," even as the writing affirms her servitude (111). Without the letter of passage, Florens is at the mercy of anyone who would challenge her journey. When the visitors to Widow Ealing's house take away the letter to "consult and pray" about whether Florens is the "Black Man's minion," she feels the full force of the letter's loss: "With the letter,

I belong and am lawful. Without it I am a weak calf abandon[ed] by the herd, a turtle without shell, a minion with no telltale signs but a darkness I am born with ...." (115).

Back within the bounds of the Vaark farm, Florens' final act in *A Mercy* is to create her own text, telling her story on the surfaces of Jacob Vaark's "profane monument to himself," first writing on the floors with the "tip of a nail" until "[t]here is no more room in this room" and then continuing her "disorderly words" on the walls (160, 158). She does not present her story as a "confession" but an attempt to discover "who is responsible" for the confluence of events that have brought her to this impasse (3). "[C]an you read," she asks the free black smithy to whom she addresses her words (3). The absent man does not know the "letters of talk," nor does he know she is writing the text (160). It is not imperative, according to Florens, that anyone else read her telling: "These careful words, closed up and wide open, will talk to themselves" (161). Yet she reconsiders, thinking "[p]erhaps these words need the air that is out in the world" (161). Her orphaned text may be a testament that answers the language of the law with lawlessness—Florens suggests her words may escape the cloister of the abandoned house in the form of ash rising from a fire; she will answer lawless laws with chaos.

In *A Mercy*, through the voices of the free and unfree, Morrison presents a "trial" of the American construction of identity in a new land in which law, both man's and God's, is manipulated to privilege the trading of "conscience for coin" at the expense of a just civilization. Framing the story are the voices of Florens and her mother. As a slave, Florens has no credibility to testify as a witness to her life in any forum recognized by the political community. Her act of reducing her story to words, creating a written text in a language not her own but taught to her with sticks in sand and pebbles on rocks, is a personal task she hopes, she says, will "give me the tears I never have," to relieve the "withering inside that enslaves" (160, 158). When her creative act offers no solace she contemplates "wildness"— the fiery destruction of the temple Vaark has built and in which her life is inscribed and circumscribed. This is not a realization of the hope Florens' mother had that her child would "someday . . . make [her] way," yet it is not an unexpected outcome in a land where law operates to diminish the humanity of both slave and master. Mistress Vaark, cured of her physical malady, has become an "infidel" with her charges. In the world outside the bounds of the farm, as within its borders, laws "authorizing chaos in defense of order" breed discontent in the free as well as the fettered. On the Vaark farm as in early America, the letter of the law holds dominion over its spirit, "a wicked thing" untempered by mercy (167).

The progression of the law in *A Mercy*'s seventeenth-century Mary's Land foreshadows the race-based and permanent status of slavery in post-colonial America. First, the law protecting the "liberties of the people"—the "rights … immunities, priviledges, and free customs" of the province"—applies to "all Inhabitants … being Christians (*Slaves excepted*)" (1 Md. Arch. 41 [1639]); emphasis added); later, a law is enacted racializing slavery and rendering it a permanent state, "obliging negroes to serve durante vita" (1 Md. Arch. 526 [1671]; still later, after some slaves attempt to evade lifetime servitude by receiving baptism, the law forecloses the emancipation of any "negro slave" so baptized or Christianized (2 Md. Arch. 272 [1671]). Florens, lettered and baptized, is nonetheless unrecognized as an inhabitant, a being outside the law's privileges and protections. The province of Mary's Land, through the linguistic edifice of the law, has succeeded in "separat[ing] and protect[ing] all whites from all others forever," as Florens' new master Jacob Vaark notes (*A Mercy* 10).

Two centuries later in nineteenth-century America, *Beloved's* Sethe bears—on her body and in her psyche—the ramifications of the law set forth in the Constitution institutionalizing involuntary servitude and creating the legal fiction that a slave is but 3/5ths of a person for purposes of counting citizens for apportionment of state representation (*U.S. Constitution*, Art. 1, §2, para. 3). All "free Persons" are counted "whole," including indentured servants, excluding only Indians who are "not taxed." Blackness, therefore, is the sole determinant of the fractional count of a person. *The Federalist* 54, written by James Madison to encourage the ratification of the federal Constitution, provides a defense and justification for the 3/5ths clause and the "mixed character" of the slave (367). Madison, writing as Publius, adopts the voice of "one of our Southern brethren" to argue that slaves "partake of both qualities: being considered by our laws, in some respects, as persons, and in other respects as property" (366). While the slave may be "compelled to labor," "vendible by one master to another," "restrained in his liberty and chastised in his body," still the slave is "protected … in his life and limbs, against the violence of others" and is "regarded by the law as a member of society, not as a part of the irrational creation; as *a moral person*, not as a mere article of property" (366–67; emphasis added).

The use of the term "moral person" in *Federalist* 54 is telling, because the law defines such a being as a construct, not a natural person. The moral person, also termed an "artificial," "fictitious" or "juristic" person, is "a being, real or imaginary, who for the purpose of legal reasoning is treated more or less as a human being …" (*BLD* 1178). The legal fiction does not, in effect, turn a human being into divisible property, but serves, as the *fictio juris* is intended, to accomplish indirectly "by compromising expedient" what cannot be performed literally on the body (*Federalist* 54, 368). Morrison's literary reimagining of this legal conflation of human and property from the slave's perspective occurs in a scene in *Beloved* in which Sethe watches Schoolteacher's pupils prepare to list her human and animal characteristics in separate columns under the guidance of their instructor (228). Earlier, Sethe had laughed at Schoolteacher's obsession with "the measuring string," which he would "wrap all over my head, 'cross my nose, around my behind," as part of his ongoing ethnographic study of the slaves of Sweet Home (226). Now, instead of thinking "he was a fool," Sethe reflects on the implications of Mrs. Garner's less than precise definition of "characteristic"—"a thing that's natural to a thing"— in the face of Schoolteacher's lesson plan and her place as a subject in it (230).

A similar recognition scene of law's constructions, deconstructions and implications occurs in *A Mercy* when Florens, out of sight in the "closet-looking place" of Widow Ealing's house, steps out into the main room of the dwelling, where visitors react in shock—a man drops his walking stick, a woman covers her eyes and asks God for help, a young girl "wails and rocks back and forth" (107, 111). Regaining their composure, they begin to discuss with Widow Ealing Florens' most startling feature—her blackness—as if she were not standing physically before them but rather existed as a terrifying figment of their collective imagination. "Afric and much more," one visitor characterizes her, assuming Florens is not only property and a human slave but the minion of a supernatural being (111). "Afric," spoken as an epithet, marks her separation from the civilized people assessing her. Her letter of passage, legal proof of her authorization to seek the blacksmith, is not sufficient evidence for the village's representatives, who must examine Florens' naked body coolly "across distances without recognition" of her humanity, less engaged than when "[s]wine look at me ... when they raise their heads from the trough" (113).

The "double character" of the slave as both property and person, as institutionalized by law, has been addressed by scholars elsewhere.[2] My interest here is in narrowing the focus of law's figurative rending of the slave into part property and part person to an examination of the way in which the law defines the notion of domicile—the place one belongs—and how the slave constructs physical and psychic spaces for herself to reconstruct an identity decreated by the force of law as she seeks a place, concrete or imaginative, where she can transmute the legal conception of freedom into a spiritual emancipation.

What Morrison has called "the hunger for a permanent place" haunts Florens and Sethe in the course of their narratives as they seek to escape "the withering inside that enslaves" (*Conversations* 50; *A Mercy* 160). Houses are rarely—and then only temporarily—homes in *A Mercy* and *Beloved*; more often, the physical structures of the master's manor and the slave's dwelling alike function as concrete manifestations of the law of slavery. Each form of "shelter" has been built and sustained under the sanction of that law, and each is haunted by it.[3] A slave, by virtue of chattel law, has no right of possession in either material things or her own life and liberty. Her "place of residence" in legal terms is designated by operation of law—where her master dwells, so dwells she. The legal understanding of "domicile" contemplates the physical presence of a person together with her intent to remain in that place; this domicile remains fixed even if she at times resides elsewhere but returns (*BLD* 523). The slave, not being *sui juris* [independent], takes on the domicile of the master. In this way, the law of slavery deprives the slave of both the legal right of possession of property and the personal right of self-possession. Whiteness itself is the prerequisite to the right of ownership—of both tangible things and one's own being.[4]

In *A Mercy* and *Beloved*, Morrison explores the implications of this racialization of the concept of domicile, that term "so closely connected with the idea of home" (Joseph H. Beale, qtd. in *BLD* 523). The first dwelling appearing in *A Mercy* is Senor D'Ortega's ostentatious Virginia plantation Jublio. Built by slaves and separated from the slave quarters by an iron gate and fence, Jublio's manor house is deemed "grandiose" and "prideful" by Jacob Vaark, but the northern farmer cannot resist envying "the house, the gate, the fence" (15, 27). What separates Vaark from D'Ortega, the former realizes, is "only things, not bloodlines or character" (27). Because Vaark is white, male and can possess, he determines to construct his own edifice, assuring himself that it will not be as "ornate" or rife with "pagan excess" as D'Ortega's Jublio, which is "compromised" by its construction and maintenance by the labor of slaves (27). Vaark differentiates himself from D'Ortega by rationalizing that his third and final house will be "pure, noble even," absent of the physical presence, the "intimacy of slave bodies"; yet, he finances the estate with "a remote labor force in Barbadoes" (19). Vaark's "noble" sentiments are belied by the "profane monument to himself" that arises on his land to displace the second, serviceable house all its dwellers find adequate but its master (44). "Sir's foolish house" is his intended residence, but his death forecloses his establishment of domicile there as well as that of all those women—Rebekka, Florens, Lina, Sorrow—whose legal status depends on Vaark's continuing existence (44). The house—unpeopled—takes on the aura of a post-lapsarian Edenic space, behind a "sinister gate" topped with two forged copper snakes; with empty windows opening out, awaiting a glazier; and without a master as Sir, having demanded that his women drag him here from his deathbed, dies in the front hall, his face shielded from the rain "blowing through the window space" (89). Sir's attempt to fulfill the noble possibilities he imagines are presented to him by his inherited patroonship in the New World succeeds only in exposing the taint of that society by its legal exploitation of the dispossessed. Never lived in, though haunted by Sir after his death, the structure becomes the canvas on which Florens inscribes her "telling" of her life in a colony peopled by the free and the unfree (157). Lawless herself, she smites Sir's monument with letters carved into the floors and walls of his great house, an appropriation of his most prized possession, repossessed by Florens for her own self-engendering, creative purposes.

For Florens, as for the slaves of *Beloved*, home is a fluid, contingent place, marked not by mortar, stone or plank, but by the manifestation or possibility of self-reclamation, either within a community or within one's own mind. "Home" is the place where ownership "of the freed self" can be claimed, and self-possession acquired (*Beloved* 112). Number 124 Bluestone Road, Cincinnati, Ohio, is a slate-gray, four-room house, but it is not a home possessed by its inhabitants; it is a place that possesses, that Denver considers "a person rather than a structure" (35). It is not a "normal house," in which its dwellers establish a legal residence with intent to stay. Denver says "I can't live here" of the house that is bereft of the community of others (49, 17) and the Clearing, both of which once brought solace to the greater community through Baby Suggs's ministrations, and which are alive with the grievances, the "venom," of Beloved (105). Number 124 was once "a cheerful, buzzing house," and it was in front of "*that* 124" where Sethe climbed down from the wagon to spend 28 days of "unslaved life" (102; 111). Sethe's reclamation of herself there was possible, but thwarted by Schoolteacher and his minions who arrived to repossess both her and her children, deemed chattel born of the mother.

Number 124—spiteful, loud, or quiet—is not only a structure haunted by slavery, possessed by a ghost seeking to understand her own passing, but a piece of real property subject to the desires or caprices of its owners, the Bodwins, by whose consent Sethe and Denver dwell within. The lives of mother and daughter, legally emancipated, remain circumscribed by others' control of their dwelling place. Sethe's hope to lay Baby Suggs to rest in the Clearing is "prevented by some rule the whites had invented about where the dead should rest" (201). The Bodwins determine to sell 124, a house "full of trouble," "desolate and exposed" since "whiteboys pulled [the fence] down, yanked up the posts and smashed the gate" (311; 192). It is Denver, at last, who exits the unfenced yard to summon the help of the community, the neighborhood women who once gathered at the Clearing with Baby Suggs. Earlier, when Paul D had suggested to Sethe that she leave 124's haunting, she was angered by his implication that leaving a house "was a little thing—a shirtwaist or a sewing basket you could walk off from or give away any old time" (26–27). Even without the physical presence of a house, Sethe does not believe that it or any other place can be expunged from memory: "Places, places are still there. If a house burns down, it's gone, but the place—the picture of it—stays, and not just in my rememory, but out there, in the world" (43). Sweet Home, its very name smiting all who lived there, has a continuing power to entrap Sethe in its fixed identity of her as part human and part domestic animal.

What Sethe comes to understand through her struggles at 124 Bluestone is that the freedom of self-possession—"claiming ownership of that freed self"—cannot be found within the confines of tangible habitations, but only within the narrative or linguistic reclamations of the self created to rewrite the law's imposed identity—one's own story. When the neighborhood women approach 124 Bluestone at Denver's request, Sethe has a vision of the Clearing "as though [it] had come to her with all its heat and simmering leaves, where the voices of women searched for the right combination, the key, the code, the sound that broke the back of words" (308). The women's singing is a "wave of sound," breaking over Sethe as if "baptiz[ing] her] in its wash," so that she can recognize what heretofore has been obscured—Schoolteacher changed her, and she must reclaim herself (308).

In *A Mercy*, Florens is convinced of the necessity of telling her story as a means of reclaiming herself "[f]rom all those who believe they have claim and rule" over her (157). Although her inscription of that story, scratched with a nail on the floor and walls of Sir's third house, does not "give [her] the tears" she had hoped for, Florens continues the telling until "the lamp burns down" (158). Then, she sleeps "among [her] words," choosing to lay her head down in a space prohibited to her by her now-crazed mistress (158). Morrison has said, "Word-work is sublime ... because it is generative" ("Nobel Lecture" 203). Florens epitomizes this cognitive assertion of self, appropriating the dead master's edifice to create a "talking room" responding to his grandiose vision for himself built by human chattel he has exploited for his own gain. The telling is neither curative nor redemptive in itself; in fact, it may lead to "wildness"—a lawless response to the institutionalized bonds of slavery— as Florens contemplates sending her words into the air as ashes along with Sir's "big, awing house" (160). The destruction of Sir's unconscious monument to slavery, whether by fire or by Florens' lettered deconstruction, is a necessary counternarrative to the authoritative voice of the law that has made the soles of Florens' feet as "hard as cypress" and Sethe's back a "revolting clump of scars" (*A Mercy* 161; *Beloved* 26). Both the "wrought-iron maze" of Sethe's back and the iron gate topped with snakes guarding Vaark's unpeopled house are the physical manifestations of a linguistic edifice built by the nation's laws binding the history of slave and master together in its horrors, and from which neither can be easily emancipated.

Notes

[1] In *Home*, Morrison's latest novel (2012), Rev. John Locke, who helps the Korean War veteran Frank Money after his escape from a hospital, tells him: "Custom is just as real as law and can be just as dangerous" (19). Rev. Locke is warning Money about travelling through northern states with no openly discriminatory laws. Morrison's choice of name for the reverend is perhaps telling: the philosopher John Locke (1632–1704) declared, "every man has a property in his own person: this nobody has any right to but himself" (Second Treatise, §27). Money's new friend is acknowledging the reification of whiteness and the consequent conversion of any other racial identity as suspect and illegitimate whether so categorized by force of law or habit.

[2] See, for example, Malick W. Ghachem's "The Slave's Two Bodies: The Life of an American Legal Fiction," *William and Mary Quarterly*, 3rd Series, 60 (4) (2003): 809–842, especially n. 6.

[3] This haunting continues in *Home* in the twentieth century, when Frank Money remembers his family being driven from their Texas home: "[B]eing outside wasn't necessary for legal or illegal disruption. You could be inside, living in your own house for years, and still, men with or without badges but always with guns could force you … to pack up and move …" (9). A house, a building for habitation, is not a home, a place of belonging, when legitimacy is not conferred on the dweller within. This sense of displacement is echoed in the opening poem of the novel: "Whose house is this? / Say, who owns this house? / It's not mine … / Say, tell me, why does its lock fit my key?"

[4] See Cheryl I. Harris, "Whiteness as Property," in *Harvard Law Review* 106 (8) (1993): 1707–1791, for an extensive examination of this subject.

Works Cited

Black's Law Dictionary. Ed. Bryan A. Garner. 8th ed. St. Paul: Thomson/West, 2004.

Catterall, Helen Tunnicliff. *Judicial Cases Concerning American Slavery and the Negro*. Vol. I, IV. Washington, D.C.: Carnegie Institution, 1937.

Hamilton, Alexander, James Madison & John Jay. *The Federalist, or The New Constitution*. 1787–88. New York: Heritage P, 1945. Print.

Harris, Cheryl I. "Whiteness as Property." *Harvard Law Review* 106 (8) (1993): 1707–1791. Print.

Locke, John. *Two Treatises of Government and a Letter Concerning Toleration*. Ed. Ian Shapiro. New Haven: Yale UP, 2003. February. Web (accessed May 24 2012).

Maryland Archives: Assembly Proceedings, 1: 41 (1639); 1: 526 (1671); 2: 272 (1671).

Morrison, Toni. *Beloved*. New York: Vintage-Random, 2004. Print.

—. *Home*. New York: Knopf, 2012. Print.

—. "Home." *The House That Race Built*. Ed. Wahnema Lubiano. New York: Pantheon, 1997. 3–12. Print.

—. Interview by Lynn Neary. "Toni Morrison Discusses *A Mercy*." Natl. Public Radio, 17 November 2008.

NPR.org. Web. 28 Dec. 2009.

—. *A Mercy*. New York: Knopf, 2008. Print.

—. "Nobel Lecture." *What Moves at the Margin*. Ed. Carolyn C. Denard. Jackson: UP of Mississippi, 2008. 198–207. Print.

—. *Playing in the Dark: Whiteness and the Literary Imagination*. 1992. New York: Vintage-Random, 1993. Print.

—. *Toni Morrison: Conversations*. Jackson, Mississippi: UP of Mississippi, 2008. Print.

Toomer, Jeanette. "Literary Giant Toni Morrison Empowers 'Voices' of Past at 92nd Street Y." *New York Amsterdam News*, December 18, 2008. 99.52:21. Web.

U.S. Constitution, Art. I, §2.

Wiecek, William M. "The Origins of the Law of Slavery in British North America," 17 *Cardozo Law Review* 1711 (May 1996).

PART III:

'TO BE FEMALE IN THIS PLACE IS TO BE AN OPEN WOUND THAT CANNOT HEAL': MEMORY, TRAUMA, AND MATERNAL LOSS

CHAPTER FIVE

'TO BE ONE OR TO HAVE ONE': 'MOTHERLOVE' IN THE FICTION OF TONI MORRISON

TERRY OTTEN

Although Toni Morrison entitled her eighth novel *Love,* all her texts embrace love as a thematic concern, its persistence and its ambiguity, its potential for generating uncompromised compassion and unrestrained violence. In a 1978 interview, Morrison confessed that all her novels are about love, "All about love . . . people do all sorts of things under its guise"; and, she concluded, "With the best intentions in the world we can do enormous harm . . . lovers and mothers and fathers and sisters."[1]

Morrison's evolving oeuvre not only takes up the issue of love, it also seeks to fathom its destructive potential in various forms – between man and woman, friends and lovers, sisters and brothers, and, perhaps most powerfully and paradoxically, parent and child. What can be more excruciating than the ironically named Cholly Breedlove raping the child he loves? Morrison insists that "I want you to look at him and see his love for his daughter and his powerlessness to help her pain. By that time, his embrace, the rape is all the gift he has left."[2] Or what of Eva Peace's remarkable expression of devastating love when she burns to death her beloved but nonfunctioning son Plum after she makes a painful journey on her crutches down the stairs and to his room, where she holds Plum in her arms and rocks him while she raises "her tongue to the edge of her lip to stop the tears from running into her mouth"?[3]

Consider, also, Ruth Foster's attempt to establish "parental" love with her father, when, at sixteen, she insists that he "plant a kiss on her lips" each night when she goes to bed and responds with "an ecstasy inappropriate to the occasion."[4] Then, too, Milkman learns from his father that Ruth enters her dead father's bed the day he died: "Naked as a yard dog, kissing him. Him dead and white and puffy and skinny, and she had her fingers in his mouth" (73). Love and its lack can lead to its distortion, as Milkman discovers again when he learns that Ruth goes to "lay down" at her father's grave six or seven times a year in an attempt to find the love her father denied. In contrast, there is the love of the extraordinary Pilate, who, like the first mother Eve, lacks a navel but possesses a love absolutely inclusive. She cries out when she dies, "I wish I'd a knowed more people. I would of loved 'em all. If I'd a knowed more, I would a loved more" (336).

Although love is often restorative and transcendent, various vagaries of love find voice in one form or the other in all of Morrison's novels. Sometimes love is cruel and pernicious. It is the "tough love" of mother for child that finds most powerful expression in Morrison's work; however, it is at the same time a force so absolute that it forbids nothing, manifesting itself in startling acts disguised by cruelty. Indeed, Morrison's novels seem to include as many orphans, abandoned, and maimed children as Ibsen's plays, but the defining nature of mother love perhaps most distinguishes her work. In *Tar Baby,* Ondine explains to Jadine that Margaret Street "loved" her son Michael even though she stuck pins in him and burned his flesh with cigarettes when he was a child. The near perversity of mother love resurfaces as well in later works like *Jazz,* in which various betrayals of mother love become assertions of its need. True Belle substitutes her love for Violet's mother for her love of her white mistress's "golden" son; and Violet learns from her mother Rose Dear's suicide "never to have children" for fear of betrayal, just as Joe vainly seeks in the young Dorcas to recover the mother love Wild denies him. Violet, after three miscarriages and a commitment not to give birth to a child in the city, is so possessed by mother love that she sleeps with a doll and finds in Dorcas the child she never bore, even while she attempts to stab her corpse at the funeral home. Joe all but unconsciously shoots Dorcas, "a girl young enough to be that daughter," while Violet wonders, "Was she the woman who took the man, or the daughter who fled her womb?"[5] Love of mother for child or its denial becomes a sustaining theme in the later novels *Paradise* and, of course, the enigmatic *Love* as well.

The nine named parts of *Paradise*, each bearing a woman's name, suggest the nine months of pregnancy, perhaps a projection of female consciousness like the twenty-eight sections of *Beloved* which mirrors the female cycle. Tales of mother love, with all its varying themes, its possessiveness, and often terrifying power, interweave each of the narratives, as in the hands of Billie Delia when she slams her daughter's head with an iron and "licked her bottom lip, tasted salt and wondered who exactly the tears were for," an echo of Pilate's weeping sorrow when she kills her son.[6]

Morrison's most recent novel *Home* extends her depiction of female consciousness in extraordinary ways, and its incorporation of mother love tests gender barriers perhaps more than any text, even given its male protagonist. The vicious grandmother Lenore's telling observation that "the four-year-old [Frank Money] was clearly the real mother" to his infant sister Cee finds credence when he returns home from the Korean War traumatized by Post Traumatic Stress Disorder to rescue her from the diabolical Dr. Beauregard Scott.[7] Frank calls her "*my only family*" (103) and "*the first person I ever took responsibility for*" (104). Cee's pregnant mother Ida had thought her unborn daughter "*more important*" than the "*kettles, canning jars, and bedding*" left behind to escape Bandera County, Texas, in Mr. Gardener's car (39); but Cee's love for her own would-be-daughter and Frank's love for his sister and her unborn proves even more insistent. Finding the sexually mutilated Cee at Scott's house, Frank "cradled her in his arms" (112), a motherly gesture he also enacted when he held his dying "brothers" Mike and Stuff in Korea. Denied her motherhood by Scott's abuses, Cee weeps for the unborn daughter who "picked me to be born to" and senses her presence "in the air, in this house" (131). As she envisions and yearns for her unborn child, Frank finds himself weeping for the scavenging Korean girl he shot during the war and discovers "*a place I didn't know was in me*" (134), an expression of love he shares with the Korean civilians he recalls who "*would (and did) die to defend their children*" (95). As he acts to defend Cee and her wished-for daughter, he again sees the girl in Korea. Taking Cee back to the place in Lotus, Georgia where they as children watched the burial of a dying man who sacrificed his life for his son, Frank gives symbolic birth to his true self. He carries the long buried man's bones wrapped in the quilt made by Cee "in his arms," as he had carried his sister and embraced his dying comrades. When Cee at last touches his shoulder and calls "Frank," it marks a coming "home," the birth of a new self: "Here Stands A Man" (145). Transcending gender, Frank is redeemed by consuming love, especially mother love, expressed in his own commitment to Cee, in her burning desire "to have one," in the Korean parents who "*would (and did) die to defend their* children," and in the "gentleman" willing to die for his son in the dark woods in Lotus.

The likely journey "to be one or to have one" likely finds fullest expression, however, in *A Mercy*, which connects directly to her most acclaimed work, *Beloved,* as an insightful and frightening depiction of the capacity of mother love to generate paradoxically brutal acts of uncompromised compassion in a world warped and distorted by a slave culture. Virtually all the mother-child relationships in *Beloved* bear the consequences of slavery. The aptly named Baby Suggs knows that her son Halle will bear the price of her freedom. Although the Garner's seem especially kind slave owners, like Jacob and Rebekka in *A Mercy*, Baby Suggs sees them as "owners" nonetheless. She tells the Garner's that now that her son has bought her freedom, "you got my boy and I'm all broke down. You be renting him out to pay for me way after I'm gone to glory."[8] With her "great heart" she rejects allegiance to the organized church too often hostage to the system that denies her all her children but Halle, just as in *A Mercy* Rebekka disdains the Anabaptists for their refusal to baptize Patrician and their "shutting her children out of heaven." In the same work, Lina recognizes that her conversion to Presbyterianism fails to "take hold," and the church "abandons her without so much as a murmur of farewell."[9] Her native wisdom is not unlike that of Baby Suggs, or other Black "Ancestors" in Morrison's novels—Eva Peace or Pilate or Thérèse similarly "must defy the system . . . provide alternative wisdom, and establish and maintain and sustain generations in the land."[10] They struggle to preserve the "tribe," the family above all else, against the corrosive culture that dominates them.

Sethe's horrific act of infanticide fully exposes the deleterious effect of such tyranny. We know, of course, that infanticide, especially of mulatto children fathered by white owners, was not uncommon among the slaves. Sethe's mother, Nan engaged in such acts. Nan tells her that her mother "threw them all away but you. . . . You she gave the name of a black man. She put her arms around him" (62). And even Ella recalls giving birth to a "white" infant after being raped by her owner and his son, and confesses, "She had delivered, but would not nurse, a hairy white thing, fathered by 'the lowest yet'" (258-59). By comparison, Sethe's act is the more terrifying, slaughtering the very child she loves in order to save it. "Motherhood," John Updike observes, "is a force in Morrison's universe as to be partly malevolent."[11]

Although both *Beloved* and *A Mercy* take place in a period of slavery, *A Mercy* is set in the late seventeenth-century and explores the founding period of an American society rooted in a capitalistic system of oppression, encompassing not only Black but European and Native victims as well. They are all orphans, Lina realizes in *A Mercy*: "Cut loose from the earth's soil, they insisted on purchases of its soil, and like all orphans they were insatiable" (54). Jacob Vaark is orphaned early as a result of his mother's death in childbirth. She was "a girl of no consequence," and his father "left him with a name easily penned and a cause of deep suspicion"

(32-33). Although he convinces himself that he is unlike other Europeans caught up in slavery, he falls prey to its nefarious appeal. He rejects D'Ortega's blatant rapacity, boasting that he rescues Sorrow "without trading his conscience for coin" (28), but he purchases Lina "outright and deliberately" and accepts Florens in payment of twenty pieces of eight. Finally, he succumbs to the lure of the slave culture and comes to envy "the house, the gate, the fence" at Ortega's pretentious estate. Though once "content to be a farmer," he adopts the capitalistic vision that distorts the values and subverts the very family he seeks. Scully, too, is yet another orphan. His mother is "sent off to the colonies for 'lewdness and disobedience'" (57). Following her death on a tavern floor when Scully is twelve, his supposed father sells him to the synod where the Anglican curate violates the youthful Scully.

All cultures participate in a "violent system," which, Morrison insists, produces an "all-consuming effort to love something well."[12] In *Beloved*, Morrison comments, she tries to give voice to the "interior" selves of slaves "in order to rip [the] veil drawn over proceedings too terrible to relate."[13] The same can be said of *A Mercy*, as she attempts to expose "unspeakable thoughts unspoken" in shifting points of view and narrative reconstructions of time. Valerie Babb notes that in *A Mercy*, "We can conceive of Morrison as a founding mother, proffering the mercy of correcting a flawed historical record, engaging the past to go beyond it."[14] In it we witness the loss of mother love in not only the central Black figures but in other mother/child relationships scarred by the corrupted system.

In *Beloved,* the "effort to love" in "a capitalistic system of oppression" accounts for Sethe's willingness to kill her child. Sethe dramatically magnifies her mother love when she lays claim to her children. She tells Paul D that freedom has released her power to love: "Look like I loved em more after I got here. Or maybe I couldn't love em proper in Kentucky because they wasn't mine to love" (162). As Morrison explains to Marsha Darling, Sethe "*became* a mother" and could "claim responsibility for her children" once she crossed over into freedom.[15] Sethe's greatest escape from slavery, Jan Furman concludes, "is [her] emphatic rejection of slavery's power to circumscribe her motherhood."[16] Sethe justifies her "rough love" and offers no apology because it "was right," she insists, "because it came from true love" (251). In a 1987 interview Morrison says of Sethe's brutal act that it was "absolutely the right thing to do"— then added, "but she had no right to do it."[17]

The gentle Paul D struggles to understand Sethe's frightening mother love. He reflects a slave mentality when he analyzes his own strategy for survival: "[Y]ou protected yourself and lived small. . . . to get to a place where you could love anything you choose . . . well now, *that* was freedom" (162). In *A Mercy,* Florens wonders what freedom is but never secures the love Paul D finds in Sethe. Yet even to the end, Paul D fears Sethe's unrestrained capacity to love her children. He fears the danger in "a used-to-be slave" loving "anything that much . . . especially if it were her own children she had settled on to love" (45).

The yearning for mother love surfaces in a different perspective in *A Mercy* and extends the theme in the compelling stories of Rebekka, Lina, Sorrow, and Florens—all mothers or would-be mothers motivated by an uncompromising need "to have or to be one." As Valerie Babb notes, all the women in the novel are acquired by transactions: "Vaark buys Lina; Rebekka becomes his wife through his funding an arranged marriage; Vaark acquires Florens in a settlement of a debt; Vaark receives Sorrow free of charge in order to remove her from the sons of a local sawyer."[18] Here, too, a "violent system" generates an "all-consuming effort to love something well." Mother love or the lack of it is similarly apparent, but no one finally shatters the "mind-forged manacles" that entrap the characters. Lina recognizes her own victimization, and with her native wisdom of bonding to the land observes that "Cut loose from the earth's soil, they insisted on purchase of its soil, and like all orphans they were insatiable" (54). Indeed, all the characters are compelled by love, and the oppressive system frustrates all their quests. Rebekka, especially, yearns for her lost children because her parents fail to love her. Her mother substitutes love "for religious matters" and treated her "with glazed indifference." If her mother objects to the union with Jacob, it "was not for love or need of her daughter, but because the husband-to-be was a heathen living among savages" (74). When Rebekka is "sold" by her father and, like those on slave ships, suffers a terrible passage to the New World to fulfill her arranged marriage with Jacob, she watches with obvious envy the prostitute Lydia and her child, Patty. Later, living with Jacob after the death of her four infants and Patrician, she "held a personal grudge" against the religious believers because each time one of her infants died, "she told herself it was anti-baptism that enraged her. But the truth was she could not bear to be around their undead, healthy children" (92). Then after Jacob—himself "a ratty orphan"--dies, her "sweet heart" succumbs to cruelty and despair: she beats Sorrow and rejects her newborn baby, takes down the faithful Lina's hammock, and tries to sell Florens.

Lina's tale is yet another tale of orphanage. When Lina is a child, smallpox devastates her tribe, and soldiers burn down her village. She, too, endures violation, raped "under a Europe's rule," and in revenge places the heads of two roosters in her lover's shoes.   When the Presbyterians sell her to Jacob, she attempts to assume a mother's role with Florens when Florens arrives at Jacob's place.   There she and Florens bond like mother and child, linked by "Mother-hunger—to become one or have one—both of them were reeling from that longing" (63). Ultimately, Lina's loss of mother love drives her to destroy Sorrow's baby.   So desperate is Lina's love of Florens as her child, she feels threatened and commits infanticide like Sethe in *Beloved*, drowning Sorrow's newborn infant.   Indeed, in Morrison's novel, European, Native, Black—all bear the loss of mother love created by the rapacity and inhumanity of a slave-driven culture. As Maxine Montgomery notes in the introduction to this collection, Morrison's later works reflect her "increasingly global narrative project involving an evacuation of America's racial past," and *A Mercy* "represents her efforts at upsetting race in ways that complicate fundamental concerns throughout her cannon." Mother love is such an integrating theme, and no figures suffer more than Sorrow and Florens.

The motherless Sorrow's supposed father captained a ship where he "reared her not as a daughter but as a sort of crewman-to-be . . . . with one important skill, patching and sewing sailcloth" (127). When he dies after the ship wrecks, Sorrow alone survives, only to be rescued by the sawyer, whose impotent wife brutalizes her and whose two sons rape her "behind the wood pile."   To survive her painful journey, Sorrow evokes her double, Twin, when she awakes from an opium dream on the wrecked ship; and she depends upon her other until she gives birth to her own daughter.   "Always an easy harvest," Sorrow seems ever to be pregnant but yet without gaining motherhood. When the jealous Lina, desperate to secure Florens as her child, learns of Sorrow's pregnancy after Jacob brings her to the farm, she fears "this one would not die" (56) and, after telling Sorrow that "the birth came too soon," she drowns the newborn infant, even though "Sorrow thought she saw her . . . newborn yawn." She "never forgot the baby breathing water every day, every night, down all the streams of the world" (124). Though she lacks a mother, Sorrow very much wants "to be one." Despite her enigmatic nature and bizarre past, motherhood transforms her into a character absolutely determined to nurture and protect her infant. When she gives safe birth to a daughter with the help of Scully and Willard, she lays claim to a transcendent motherhood. Having done "something, something important, by herself" (133), she becomes another fierce mother, like Sethe when she crosses the river into freedom. Twin disappears as Sorrow proudly presents herself to her baby: "'I am your mother,' she said. 'My name is Complete'" (134).

Once she can truly call herself mother, she feels empowered. As Andrea O'Reilly notes, "Morrison defines and positions maternal identity as a site of power for women."[19] Scully notes that "she glowed" when pregnant, and Florens clearly sees the transformation, commenting, "Sorrow is a mother. Nothing more nothing less" (159). Her claim of motherhood marks the culmination of her personal journey from rejected daughter to empowerment. To her, the "baby came first and she would postpone egg-gathering, delay milking, interrupt any field chore if she heard a whimper from the infant always somewhere near" (146).

It is Florens' "mother-hunger—to be one or have one" that provides the structural spine of the novel, however, and her story incorporates the central common quest of the other women characters to gain or be a mother. When Jacob brings Florens home, she triggers a search for mother love. Rebekka gives Florens her dead daughter's shoes in a vain attempt to somehow reconnect with Patrician, and Lina embraces Florens as her own child. Pained by her own mother's seeming rejection of her, Florens treasures Lina's stories evoking the love of mother for child: "Especially called for were stories of mothers fighting to save their children from wolves and natural disasters" (61), the reflection of a mother's struggle to protect her own child above all else. We can see reflected in this Sethe's willingness to save Beloved even by slaying her. When Florens later sets out to find the blacksmith to heal the dying Rebekka, she naively asks the slaves on the Ney brothers' wagon, "are you leaving someone dear behind?" which leads one of them to call her "Daft" (40). He shares Paul D's strategy of parental survival in the midst of slavery: "to love just a little bit, so when they broke its back, or shoved it in a cracker sack, well, maybe you'd have a little love left over for the next one" (45).

Before she sets out to find the blacksmith, Florens wonders what freedom is. "I don't know the feeling of or what it means, free and not free. But I have a memory." Suddenly on her own and for the moment without chains, she feels "A little scare of this looseness. Is this how free feels? I don't like it" (69-70). Her harrowing journey recalls Beloved's account of the slave ship and becomes for her a painful passage of recognition and, finally, a measure of freedom. To be sure, she owes much to what she learns from Lina's Indian awareness as well as to her own African past and the kindness of others. After she receives the help of the Indian men on horseback who offer her food and water, she comes to Widow Ealing's house where she once again confronts the potential treachery of mother love. The Widow lashes her own daughter Jane's legs to prove she bleeds and is therefore not a demon. Like Rebekka's mother,

the Widow embraces her perverse religion more than her child. The
fanatical believers threaten Florens, and the young woman comes to
recognize her state. She recalls her own mother, whose words she strains
to hear: ". . . I am a weak calf abandoned by the herd, a turtle without a
shell, a minion with no telltale signs, but a darkness I am born with,
outside, yes, but inside as well and the inside darkness is small, feathered
and toothy. Is that what my mother knows? Why she chooses me to live
without?" (115). Thinking of her mother even as she travels to find the
blacksmith, she reflects, "If my mother is not dead she can be telling me
these things" (109). The search for the blacksmith encompasses the quest
for her mother.

Florens reaches the blacksmith's home only to find herself once again
rejected for another child. Seeing the foundling child Malaik recalls her
own mother "holding her little boy's hand" and giving her away, and she
dreams that her mother "is standing by [the blacksmith's] cot and this time
her baby boy is Malaik" (138). Fearing the "power" in the doll Malaik
carries, she takes it and puts it high on a shelf, only later to project herself
onto it as a child abandoned "in a corner like a precious child no person
wants" (139). And when the blacksmith returns and chooses Malaik
instead of her because she is "nothing but wilderness" and "a slave by
choice," she feels something paradoxical: "I am living the dying inside.
Now. Not again. Feathers lifting. I unfold" (142). Earlier she had
wondered "how free feels," now, ironically, she gains an anguished
freedom from the blacksmith or any owner to find "Me"—a bittersweet
victory at best.

When Florens' mother speaks in the penultimate last section of the
novel, Florens cannot hear her words, but her mother's poignant gesture of
love leads to her daughter's discovery of self and a measure of release.
However unknowingly, she gives truth to her mother's claim that "to give
yourself to another is a wicked thing" (167). Although slave traders rape
the mother in the curing shed "to break we in," her mother will save her
daughter at any cost. Just as Sethe declares "if I hadn't killed [Beloved]
she would have died" (200), Florens' mother knows that "There is no
protection" for her daughter unless she sacrifices her. She sees that
Florens' breasts "are rising too soon" and that "You caught Senhor's eye"
(166). The mother is willing to endure the rape "because the results were
you and your brother" (160), but she will not see her daughter violated. In
much the same way that Sethe claims Beloved, the mother finds Florens
"the best part of herself," a self freed not only from physical slavery but
the mental chains that create her internal "Darkness." It is "the only thing
to do." "It wasn't a miracle" bestowed by God, she insists, but "a

memory" (166-67). If Sethe's horrific deed could stop Schoolteacher in his tracks, Florens' mother's act could free her daughter as well—"In full . . . . Slave. Free. I last" (161). Regretfully, Florens realizes that "I cannot know what my mother is telling me. Nor can she know what I am wanting to tell her" (161), but she gains a victory, nonetheless. Cheryl Miller, who, along with other reviewers, finds the ending of the novel strained or incomplete, writes that Florens "purges her pain through the act of writing" on the walls of Jacob's house, but it "focused on her own hurts and remains locked in the 'darkness' of her own mind."[20] In a way, though, the seeming irresolution points to the realization Sethe ultimately achieves in a world that slavery shapes.

The capitalistic system which enslaves, barters, sells, and breeds women in *A Mercy* seems so ingrained in Sethe's world that only the most horrendous of acts can allow her to truly possess her child. Whereas in *A Mercy* Florens' mother accepts the violation that the mother faces because Florens and her brother are the result, Sethe reaches the height of her mother love only after she leaves Sweet Home and gives birth to Denver. Although born in slavery, Beloved demands absolute love when Sethe crosses over with her into freedom. If, as Claudia says in *The Bluest Eye,* "the love of a free man is never safe" (206),[21] then the love of a freed mother is the most dangerous love of all.

Sethe is separated from her mother at three weeks old, not an uncommon event for slave children. She receives milk from another woman's breast and saw her mother only once as a hat in the rice field. Her forced separation from her mother explains why she is so driven "to get milk to my baby girl" (16) after Schoolteachers' "boys" take her milk. Sethe always carries the memory of her mother with her, just as Florens keeps dreaming of her mother's attempt to speak to her. Andrea O'Reilly aptly observes that "when Sethe is pregnant with Denver, the slave mother calls the daughter her antelope . . . the name of the dance Sethe's mother performed before she died at Sweet Home." And she adds, "Sethe wants to be a daughter to her mother, and a mother to her daughter."[22] One might note that at the end of the novel, Denver says of Sethe and Beloved, "it was difficult . . . to tell who was who" (24). For Morrison, Sethe's claim of motherhood is a political gesture, an act of defiance against a culture of repression. As Sethe declares, "I birthed them and got em out and it wasn't no accident. I did that. . . . it was the only thing I ever did on my own. Decided" (162). Rejecting Paul D's warning "Don't love her too much. Don't" (206), she opts for a mother's "too thick love."

It is little wonder that Florens confesses that "mothers nursing greedy babies scare me" (8) or that Denver is terrorized by "Something" in Sethe "that could make it all right to kill her own." As Andrea O'Reilly aptly observes, "It" is the perverse power of a slave system engendered by capitalistic greed that transfigures mother love into a potential weapon of unqualified expression, a love that can burn a son to death, or slit a baby daughter's throat – acts of appalling horror born of mercy.[23] Morrison says of her characters that they are "the combination of virtue and flaw, of good intentions gone awry, of wickedness cleansed and people made whole again. If you judge them by the best that they have done, they are wonderful. If you judge them by the worst that they have done, they are terrible."[24] The mothers in *Beloved* and *A Mercy* are capable of unqualified love often projected in seeming cruelty and violation, and the children in both novels seek above all to recover a mother love sometimes confused with malevolence. In a memorable parable-like passage in *A Mercy*, Lina tells Florens the tale of an eagle who lays her eggs in a nest high above snake and animal predators. "Her talons are sharpened on rock," she notes, and "her beak is like the scythe of a war god." Only the lust and greed of man threatens her brood. When man attacks the eagle/mother and strikes her with his stick, she falls screaming:

> "And the eggs?" she asks.
> "They hatch alone," says Lina.
> "Do they live?" Florens' whispering is urgent.
> "We have," says Lina. (62-63)

We hear the foreshadowing of this at the end of *Beloved* when Paul D assures Sethe, "You your best thing . . . you are." "Me?" she replies, "Me?" (273).

Notes

[1] Jane Bakerman, "'The Seams Can't Show': An Interview with Toni Morrison," *Black American Literature Forum* 12 (1978): 56-60.

[2] Claudia Tate, "Toni Morrison," in *Black Women Writers*, ed. Claudia Tate (New York: Continuum, 1983), 125.

[3] Toni Morrison, *Sula* (New York: New American Library, 1973), 47. As Barbara Christian claims, Plum's death is "a ritual killing inspired by love—a ritual sacrifice by fire." *Black Woman Novelists: The Development of a Tradition 1892-1976* (Westport, Ct.: Greenwood Press, 1980), 159.

[4] Toni Morrison, *Song of Solomon* (New York: A Plume Book, 1987), 23. Page numbers will be cited parenthetically in the text.

[5] Toni Morrison, *Jazz* (New York: Alfred A. Knopf, 1992), 109.

[6] Toni Morrison, *Paradise* (New York: Alfred A, Knopf, 1998), 204. One might also contrast the "love" expressed by the Rev "Take No Prisoners" Pullman with

Baby Suggs' sermon at the Clearing professing the unconditional love of her "great heart."

[7] Toni Morrison, *Home* (New York: Alfred A. Knopf, 2012), 88. Page numbers will be cited parenthetically in the text.

[8] Toni Morrison, *Beloved* (New York: Alfred A. Knopf, 1987), 146. Page references will be cited parenthetically in the text.

[9] Toni Morrison, *A Mercy* (New York: Alfred A Knopf, 2008), 49. Page numbers will be cited parenthetically in the text.

[10] Toni Morrison, "City Limits, Village Values: Concepts of the Neighborhood in Black Fiction," *Literature and the Urban Experience: Essays on the City and Literature*, ed. Michael C. Jaye and Ann Chalmers Watts (New Brunswick, N. J.: Rutgers University Press, 1981), 43.

[11] John Updike, "Dreaming Wilderness," *The New Yorker*, 3 November 2008: 113.

[12] "Toni Morrison," interview with Amanda Smith, *Publisher's Weekly*, 21 August 1987:5.

[13] Toni Morrison, "The Site of Memory," *Inventing the Truth: The Art and Craft of Memoir*, second edition, ed. William Zinnser (Boston: Houghton-Mifflin, 1995), 91.

[14] Valerie Babb, "*E Pluribus Unum*? The American Origins Narrative in Toni Morrison's *A Mercy*," MELUS, 36:2 (2011), 195. See also, Maxine Montgomery, "Got on My Traveling Shoes: Migration, Exile and Home in Toni Morrison's *A Mercy*," *Journal of Black Studies*, 42:4 (2010), 627-37.

[15] Marsha Darling, "In the Realm of Responsibility: A Conversation with Toni Morrison," *The Women's Review of Books*, March 1988, 6.

[16] Jan Furman, *Toni Morrison's Fiction* (Columbia, University of South Carolina Press, 1996), 70. As Garleen Greval notes, "The signature of a mother/child's abandonment sprawls across" both *Beloved* and *A Mercy*. Garleen Greval, review of *A Mercy*, MELUS, 36:2 (2011), 193.

[17] *MacNeil-Lehrer Newshour*, PBS, 29 September 1987.

[18] Babb, 156.

[19] Andrea O'Reilly, *Toni Morrison and Motherhood: A Politics of the Heart* (Albany: State University of New York Press, 2004), 1.

[20] Cheryl Miller, "Mine, Mine, Mine," *Commentary*, March 2009, 64.

[21] Toni Morrison, *The Bluest Eye* (New York: A Plume Book 1970), 206.

[22] O'Reilly, 87, 89.

[23] In Andrea O'Reilly's words, "Morrison articulates a fully developed theory of African-American mothering that is central to her larger political and philosophical stance on black womanhood." O'Reilly, 1. In *A Mercy*, we might add, we see her political vision of motherhood extended to other races as well.

[24] "An Interview with Toni Morrison," with Nellie McKay, *Contemporary Literature*, 24 (1983):423. Babb, Valerie. "E Pluribus Unum? The American Origins Narrative in Toni Morrison's *A Mercy*." MELUS, 36:2 (2011), 147-64.

Works Cited

Babb, Valerie. "E Pluribus Unum? The American Origins Narrative in Toni Morrison's *A Mercy.*" MELUS, 36:2 (2011), 147-64.

Bakerman, Jane. "The Seams Can't Show: An Interview with Toni Morrison." *Black American Literature Forum,* 12 (1978): 56-60.

Christian, Barbara. *Black Women Novelists: The Development of a Tradition, 1882-1976.* Westport: Greenwood Press, 1980.

Darling, Marsha. "In the Realm of Responsibility: A Conversation with Toni Morrison." *The Women's Review of Books,* March 1988, 5-6.

Furman, Jan. *Toni Morrison's Fiction.* Columbia: University of South Carolina Press, 1996.

Greval, Garleen. "Review of *A Mercy.*" MELUS, 36:2 (2011), 193.

MacNeil-Lehrer Newshour. Interview with Toni Morrison. PBS, 29 September 1987.

McKay, Nellie. "An Interview with Toni Morrison." *Contemporary Literature,* 24 (1983), 413-29.

Miller, Cheryl. "Mine, Mine, Mine." *Commentary,* March 2009, 64.

Montgomery, Maxine. "Got on my Traveling Shoes, Exile and Home in Toni Morrison's *A Mercy.*" *Journal of Black Studies*, 42:4 (2010), 627-37.

Morrison, Toni. *A Mercy.* New York: Alfred A. Knopf, 2008.

—. *Beloved.* New York: Alfred A. Knopf, 1987.

—. "City Limits Village Values: Concepts of the Neighborhood in Black Fiction." *Literature and the Urban Experience: Essays on the City and Literature.* Second Edition.
  Ed. Michael C. Jaye and Ann Chalmers Watts. New Brunswick: Rutgers University Press, 1981. 35-43.

—. *Home.* New York: Alfred A. Knopf, 2012.

—. *Jazz.* New York: Alfred A. Knopf, 1992.

—. *Paradise.* New York: Alfred A. Knopf, 1998.

—. *Song of Solomon.* New York: A Plume Book, 1987.

—. "The Site of Memory." *Inventing the Truth: The Art and Craft of Memoir.* Second Edition. Ed. William Zinnser. Boston: Houghton-Mifflin, 1955. 101-24.

—. *Sula.* New York: New American Library, 1973.

O'Reilly, Andrea. *Toni Morrison and Motherhood: A Politics of the Heart.* Albany: State University of New York Press, 2004.

Smith, Amanda. "Toni Morrison." *Publisher's Weekly*, 21 August 1987, 5.

Tate, Claudia. "Toni Morrison." *Black Women Writers at Work*. New York: Continuum, 1983. 137-31.

Updike, John. "Dreaming Wilderness." *The New Yorker*, 3 November 2008, 112-14.

CHAPTER SIX

"MOTHER HUNGER": TRAUMA, INTRA-FEMININE IDENTIFICATION, AND WOMEN'S COMMUNITIES IN TONI MORRISON'S *BELOVED, PARADISE* AND *A MERCY*

SANDRA COX

Could she sing? (Was it nice to hear when she did?) Was she pretty? Was she a good friend? Could she have been a loving mother? A faithful wife? Have I got a sister and does she favor me? If my mother knew me, would she like me?

—Beloved

She is my mother. Your mother too. Whose mother you?

—Paradise

God hated idleness most of all, so staring off into space to weep for a mother or a playmate was to court damnation.

—A Mercy

In these three epigraphs from Toni Morrison's novels maternity emerges as a nuanced site of trauma and identification. *Beloved* (1987), *Paradise* (1998) and *A Mercy* (2008) reveal the myriad ways in which the maternal role is at once both traumatic and therapeutic for the fictional characters who deal with personal and familial loss. Sethe wonders about the relationship she might have had with her lost mother. Consolata claims that maternity unites women and suggests that even without shared family history or genetics, kinship between women is founded upon a range of possible permutations of the mother-daughter dyad. In Morrison's most recent novel, Sorrow internalizes that the losses of her mother and sister are not only irrecoverable, but that her trauma is also punishable within a patriarchal colonial system.

In *Beloved,* Morrison presents female characters who are mothers to lost children, children of lost mothers or, like the titular ghost-made-flesh and the ex-slave Sethe, both. In *Paradise,* the focus on lost children and lost mothers is extended, but in different ways. Whereas *Beloved* charts the way slavery frustrates healthy maternal and filial relationships for African American women, *Paradise* contains several racially ambiguous characters collected in solidarity, which suggests that racism and patriarchy destroy American families regardless of the ethnic backgrounds of the family members. In her most recent novel, *A Mercy*, Morrison again revisits motherloss, slavery and the ways in which women succeed and fail at creating intra-feminine communities as sites of healing. The author's attention to the historicization of all three novels is evident. From the narrative of Margaret Garner as an Ur-Sethe in *Beloved,* to the Sundown towns of central Oklahoma in the antebellum period in *Paradise,* and the colonial wilderness that is the Atlantic coast in *A Mercy*, the contextual details of setting, character and plot depict African American culture and geography with a verisimilitude that represents an 'authentic' cultural history as closely as possible in testimonial fiction.

In spite of the fact that the continuity among themes contests boundaries between the three novels, there are ways to read each as a complicating response to the one that precedes it. Seeing a recursive relationship between the texts illuminates how Morrison grapples with the problem of creating community without colonization and respecting difference without creating hierarchy. Morrison implicitly posits a series of concerns about how outsider readers can interpret and respond to fictionalized testimony given by characters in *Beloved*, *Paradise* and *A Mercy*. Each novel portrays female subjects in crisis due to motherloss, but each of these crises is more than a singular instance of personal bereavement. In all three novels, motherloss is a symptom of cultural trauma. As Morrison dramatizes first-person accounts of trauma visited upon African American women's bodies she calls the reader's attention to the moral and ethical implications of these accounts, and implicitly calls for deliberation on appropriate ways to memorialize and correct the atrocities to which her characters bear witness. Each narrative provides tacit meta-commentary about how the telling of (and listening to) such acts of witness might present a mechanism for cross-cultural coalition building between women. In *Beloved* the characters demonstrate the plausibility of passing on stories as ways to heal motherloss in African American women's communities specifically. *Paradise* shows that similar possibilities might exist for inter-ethnic women's coalitions, which provide healing spaces until those spaces are infiltrated by patriarchy, and its ensuing violence. However, in *A Mercy*, Morrison seems to complicate the facility of women's communities in the earlier texts by depicting failed identification; the community of women in *A Mercy* is living without men and in a space that is at least nominally outside concretized racial hierarchies, but it does not prove a viable space in which an intrafeminine community can be therapeutic. In investigating the commonalities and differences between the three narratives one might be able to infer some claims about how these communities can succeed (as well as the reasons they fail) as a context within which to work through maternal trauma.

On Intrafeminine Community and Maternal Trauma

As the characters in *Beloved, Paradise* and *A Mercy* attempt (with varying levels of success) to build an intrafeminine community that rejects the racism of dominant American culture, so, too, must Morrison's readers, who come to find their own vexed mechanisms for identifying with characters across identity-based differences as those differences are reflected in the texts. Identity—particularly racial and gendered identity—is central to all three novels because Morrison creates and evocatively portrays paradoxically personalized (and therefore private) and politicized (and therefore public) experiences. In crafting the settings in which those traumatic experiences take place—like the all-Black neighborhood surrounding Bluestone Road in Cincinnati, the Convent outside Ruby, Oklahoma, and the Vaark patroonship in colonial Maryland—Morrison makes appeals to solidarity within and across collective identity structures. She employs narrative to speak for a collective identity to be embodied by particular and individuated characters in those spaces. However, those personal traumas rendered in *Beloved, Paradise* and *A Mercy* draw from very real touchstones for solidarity. The recurrent theme of the sexual exploitation of women of color is contextualized by calling attention to a cultural oversexualization of the black female body, which is also the site of vexed identifications for women across generational and cultural differences. In *Beloved, Paradise* and *A Mercy*, mothers are estranged from daughters and women are separated by an illusory color line, but mothers and daughters alike remain subject to sexual violence regardless of their ethnic identities.

Solidarity for any identity-based community, be it racial or gendered, is reified by testimonial prose that sees those communities as either sites of trauma—as Sweet Home, Ruby and the Spanish Planation are—or of healing—as Cincinnati, the Convent and the patroonship prove to have the potential to become. In an interview with Salman Rushdie, Morrison herself noted that: "[e]ven though one [is] working for a kind of freedom and escape ... one has to accept the fact that art is contrivance" (qtd. in Denard 52). Rushdie agrees with Morrison and even goes so far as to argue that the text of a novel is a kind of script and the writer, as much as the narrator, performs it—"the performer is also the creator" (53). To which Morrison responds, simply, "Exactly." The function of fiction here becomes performative—a text that *does* as it *is,* and *is* as it *does.* In fact, transformative reading is only plausible if one accepts the radical claim that narrative can have some subjectivity—that texts sometimes act upon their readers. The socio-political functions of such doing-and-being permit this performative function, with regard to testimonial fiction that works to represent history, and mirror the aforementioned duality in perspective that shrinks the space between groups and individuals, and between characters and readers. That complicated nexus of identity is a necessary precondition for transformative reading practices. In such a transformative moment of literary analysis, the singular becomes the plural, the specific becomes the general and the personal becomes the political; that transformative moment may be fleeting, but it may also be a mechanism for communicating across identity-based differences in ways that may garner acceptance and understanding. So when the form (a testimonial novel that speaks about history as an object of narrative transformation) undertakes a particular sort of content (the possibilities of using community to create spaces for dealing with cultural trauma) the ways in which characters (as testifying voices that speak for those communities) convey their experiences posit a metafictive statement on the viability of women's communities and racial communities to serve that transformative function for communities and individuals in crisis.

On Slavery, Kinship and *Beloved*

The American slavery system, and its enduring legacy of institutionalized racism, produced maternal pathologies for African American women, and the trauma that produces that pathology appears in the testimony delivered by Morrison's female characters. By considering how attachments between women might assuage or exacerbate that cultural trauma, Morrison investigates how the use of a testimonial narrative might work to produce a mechanism for cross-cultural communication without colonization. In *Beloved*, attachments between African American women become a potential venue for finding a cohesive sense of self, particularly after that cohesion is shattered by racially and sexually motivated experiences of violence.

However, the ways in which that intraracial community might translate to an interracial one begs a question of the ways in which readers may identify with the characters. While Morrison intends for African American women to read the text as a means of finding an absent, silenced or inaccurate cultural history, the question of whether women who do not share that cultural history will, can or should identify with those characters is a vexed one. Jean Wyatt's exploration of *Beloved* raises two important questions: "What are the identification processes that account for the transmission of trauma? … What is the identification mechanism that enables someone to suffer symptoms of a collective trauma, of a traumatic past experienced by a whole group of people, but not by the sufferer herself?" (66). Just as Denver cannot fully integrate her mother's experiences at Sweet Home with her own sense of herself as an African American woman coming of age in a free-state, so, too, might outsider readers, who have not experienced the trauma of institutionalized racism against African Americans, struggle to find ethical means of identifying with Morrison's testifying characters. Since a goal of this analysis is to find Morrison's own implicit claims about that very issue, Wyatt's inquiries serve as an apt point of entry, not just into an analysis of *Beloved* but into a larger critical consideration of the way Morrison shapes identity in specific contexts.

In the case of *Beloved*, Morrison represents the collective identity of her African-American characters as fragmented and haunted—literally and figuratively—by the incipient trauma of enslavement; Wyatt's examination seeks to explain how collective identification works within a context of cultural trauma in the cases of Sethe's relationships to her children, lovers and community. Wyatt is not the only critic to take this approach to *Beloved*. Lorraine Liscio treats Sethe's maternal relationships and notes a distinction between her concern for her female and male offspring (33). Because Sethe's traumatic experiences in the narrative find expression in terms of their embodied traces—the chokecherry scar and the theft of her milk, most obviously—the fear she feels for her daughters is a consequence of her close identification with them; she demonstrates anxiety about the distinct possibility that they too will be forced to endure such treatment. The institution of slavery makes murder the only mechanism by which Sethe is able to ensure that her infant daughter will not experience the sexual violence that Schoolteacher and his boys are certain to visit upon her if the child matures at Sweet Home. Sethe sees her own trauma—the theft of her milk, the impotence and insanity of her husband, the inevitable loss of her children—in her daughter's future. Ultimately, her decision to murder the Already-Crawling Girl is a consequence of that identification—Sethe would rather die than endure such treatment again, so the murder is an act of self-annihilation and mercy toward the infant child. Emma Parker suggests that this identification, which Sethe doesn't seem to feel for her sons Howard and Buglar, manifests a hysterical response to the oppressive nature of the historical context of the narrative.

All three critics—Wyatt, Liscio and Parker—note that the singing of the women of Bluestone Road is what finally disrupts the extreme identification between Sethe and Beloved in ways that allow Sethe to begin a process of recovering. Because Baby Suggs and the African American women in Cincinnati present a geographic and communal space that is free of the dangers Sethe would both die and kill to escape, Denver is spared her older sister's two equally horrible fates—the sexual violence of the slaveholder or the desperate homicide of the mother. Although there are ways in which Beloved's entrance complicates the safety of the intrafeminine community, Morrison manages to imagine a way for the reconnection of mother and daughter to serve as a means of successful integration into a community that assists both child and parent in dealing with—if not recovering from—the cultural trauma that slavery visits upon Sethe and her family.

In *Beloved* there are multiple layers of motherloss as an initiator of women's trauma. The links between the American slavery system and that recurring personal tragedy elevate motherloss to a cultural trauma. Sethe suffers a separation from her own mother, and struggles to forgive Halle for prioritizing his mother's freedom over that of his wife and children. Sethe also fights to remake a connection with her murdered child through her relationship with Beloved and to find a way to normalize her parenting of the surviving daughter Denver. Each of these actions is a step in a healing process that is made more fulsome and potent through the support of women's communities. The coming together of multiple generations—beginning with Denver's birth in the wilderness, which is facilitated by a wondering white woman and culminating in the singing outside 124 that literally exorcises the ghost of murdered girl children of enslaved mothers. Although Sethe cannot recover her biological mother, she does learn about those things she questions in the epigraph. When she wonders what her mother, whom she never knew, might have been like she can only create a bricolage of the women that raised her. Sethe knows about women's singing when "it [is] nice to hear," she learns about beauty and friendship, and what it means to be "a loving mother" and a "faithful wife" (163). Because of the haven that the women of Bluestone Road provide, she may even find a space to help Denver discover her sister's history and to know, and like, her mother.

On Patriarchy, Colonialism and *Paradise*

As if to further complicate the Amy Denver-Sethe interaction that provides the singular moment of intercultural community between women in *Beloved*, *Paradise* follows a handful of women of differing ethnic and racial origins in another fictional account of collective female experience. This instance of collectivization, like the singing of the women of Bluestone Road, attempts to overcome the emphatic focus on racial hierarchies by considering mothering as a universal experience that provides ground for identification across identity boundaries. In *Paradise*, Morrison investigates motherloss and women's communities further, this time considering how inter-ethnic subject positions figure in the ways in which affiliation and identification might address cultural trauma and sexual violence. Even though the contexts for maternal attachment as a point of crisis in Morrison's body of fiction are not limited to the trauma of slavery (although that trauma is certainly significant enough to produce content for a great deal of literary reflection), *Paradise* shares with *Beloved* a preoccupation with the ways in which—even after emancipation and the Great Migration—the American slavery systems continue to constrain African American familial relationships. The two novels share an attention to setting as an active character—if "124 is spiteful" then Ruby is suspicious—so the ways in which women form relationships are contextualized in the space in which those relationships evolve (*Beloved* 1). Critics have noted that *Paradise*, in particular, fashions a sense of feminist coalition that might provide a model for avoiding the polemics of a racial hierarchy. For instance, Magali Cornier Michael argues that "Morrison's *Paradise* explores coalition processes that are more accommodative, caring, and loving, rather than exploitative, and that are aimed principally at survival and at moving toward a new, alternative form of non-hierarchical justice, rather than at maximizing power and winning" (644). By de-emphasizing hierarchy the characters seek to remake maternity without any authoritarian features. As Connie suggests in the epigraph, the focus of motherhood at the Convent outside of Ruby is the production of nurture—women must come not only to feel that they are worthy of mothering, of unconditional love, but they must also cultivate a sense of responsibility, an impetus to mother other women. The outsider women come to the Convent to be mothered by (and in turn serve as mother to) Connie. After a period of healing, those same outsider women, all of disparate socio-economic and cultural backgrounds, then mother the women of Ruby who come to the Convent to escape patriarchal control. In crafting this cast of interdependent multicultural characters and examining their relationships, Morrison addresses *Paradise* to a mixed audience in her representation of inter-ethnic communities of women; the novel speaks both to African American women seeking their own places in American history and to an audience of outsiders who read over the shoulders of African American women. The narrative provides cues for attentive readers to follow that might make a fine model for intrafeminine, interracial communities.

Paradise juxtaposes two communities—the all-black town Ruby and the all-female commune the Convent. The book begins will a chilling first sentence that calls attention to the interethnic community in the Convent that will ultimately become the object of violence for the menfolk of Ruby—"They shot the white girl first" (1). The novel refuses a clear answer to the unwritten question that first line inspires—"Which girl is white?"—which points to one feature of the model Morrison seems to suggest. By refusing race as a primary identifier, by subjugating it to other, more universal female experiences (like being mothered, mothering and facing the potential of violence from men), an appropriate ground for solidarity might be found.

The first half of the novel seems to focus on revealing the problems in constructing a community based on racial-sameness, a prospect that seemed so hopeful at the end of *Beloved*. The unifying sentiment that holds the men and most upstanding women in Ruby together is a sense of shared history, racial solidarity and apprehension about the multicultural women's community that exists on the fringes of their township. The relationship between the two communities is troubled by the suspicions of the townsfolk:

> Outrages that had been accumulating all along took shape as evidence. A mother was knocked down the stairs by her cold-eyed daughter. Four damaged infants were born in one family. Daughters refused to get out of bed. Brides disappeared on their honeymoons. Two brothers shot each other on New Year's Day. Trips to Demby for VD shots became common … The proof they had been collecting since the terrible discovery in the spring could not be denied: the one thing that connected all these catastrophes was in the Convent. And in the Convent were those women. (5)

The very phrase "those women" seems to echo the not-so-veiled exclusionary sentiments that the founders of Ruby faced during their post-bellum sojourn westward. The fact is that this exclusion is causally linked to women's misbehavior, a series of "outrages" that separate daughters from mothers and brides from husbands. As in *Beloved*, the women of the Convent, and a good percentage of the women of Ruby, struggle against perceptions that they are guilty of some sort of sexual deviance. This perception often culminates for female characters in *Paradise* in some sort of physical or psychic sexual trauma—exploitative seductions, public humiliations and violent assaults.

The women, each fleeing trauma—either from sexual violence or motherloss—and finding sanctuary in the crumbling American Indian boarding school that has become Consolata's home, seem to have the potential to collectively negotiate trauma in ways that are similar to those demonstrated at the end of *Beloved*, or at least they seem to until the men of Ruby take violent action against them. Even in the wake of that violence, the women, now apparitions or against-all-odds survivors, work toward reunification with the loved-ones from whom they were estranged by trauma. Because of this ending, Morrison's implicit claim seems to suggest that patriarchal control and misogynist violence are the larger threat to women's solidarity than race-based legacies of supremacy and oppression. *Paradise* has even been read as a kind of ghost story about fallen women coming to Connie as a sort of placeholder for a lost mother or a withheld savior. Sarah Appleton Aguiar notes:

> [a]s Morrison includes in *Beloved* dead characters cohabiting with the living, the possibility that all or some of the women—Mavis, Gigi, Seneca, and Pallas—are dead before they reach the Convent is a viable one. Each has suffered tragic and potentially fatal circumstances before her arrival. Pallas has been chased and raped; maybe she has drowned. Seneca has been 'hired' by a sadistic woman to indulge her sexually violent fantasies; maybe she, too, has been murdered. Gigi participated in a riot that left at least one child dead. And maybe Mavis's husband suffocated her, or she has been murdered by the daughter who dreams apologies to her. 'Come Prepared or Not at All' can be applied to these women; if they are dead but have not 'passed on,' perhaps they are not yet prepared for death. (n. pag.)

These dead women each in turn struggle with maternity. Connie remembers how the nuns took her from her mother early in her life. Pallas, through giving birth to Divine, comes to terms with her mother's betrayal. Mavis comes to the Convent behind the wheel of the Cadillac in which her twins died. Even the living women of Ruby are marked by fraught mother-daughter tensions. Billie Delia's hatred of her mother is revealed to be a veil of self-loathing covering her sexual shame. Arnette casts forth a child willingly, undertaking to give birth prematurely. Sweetie Fleetwood longs to be free of the burden of caring for four sickly children. Seneca desperately seeks a maternal figure. The inability to negotiate motherloss may, as Agiar suggests, be a manifestation of ill-preparedness. Whether the women are ghosts or alive, the potency of their relationships to one another seems to suggest that part of 'coming prepared' means coming together.

Because all of these women—both multicultural outsiders and the African American women of Ruby—work through their trauma together, the ways in which that takes place merit a full investigation. What is immediately most obvious is that a suspension of suspicion about and judgment upon other women is the first step to successfully integrating into the community at the Convent, which in turn leads to dealing with the trauma that brings each of them to that community to begin with. The outsiders must learn to nurture one another, and this often means letting go of hierarchies. Even though class separates Seneca from Pallas outside the Convent (one is an abandoned child who has lived in abject poverty and the other the spoiled daughter of two upper middle-class professionals), the limited omniscience of the narrative style indicates to readers that each young woman slowly comes to let go of the sense of resentment and entitlement that initially keep them from being friends. The women also slowly cease to judge one another's sexual behavior. For instance, after the narrator reveals Billie Delia's public shame—that she once shed her underpants and begged to be set astride a horse in full view of all the townsfolk—the close narration from her perspective begins to let go of the condemnatory speech about the Convent women that her mother, Pat, had impressed upon her daughter.

When the women begin to come together in earnest—when even the "upright" women of Ruby begin to see the value of intrafeminine community—the men of Ruby perceive this coalition as a threat, an "outrage." Even as Morrison demonstrates the psycho-social benefits of women's communities she acknowledges that the exclusion of men breeds resentment, fear and violence from outside that community. If one resists Agiar's claims that the women at the Convent are dead, then there is no small amount of irony that the place in which each woman is able to heal from the trauma that nearly killed her is also the place in which she will be killed. The question of whether or not the attempt at producing a transformative space for intercultural intrafeminine identification without erasure is left open in *Paradise*, even as the apparitional characters seem to make peace with their loved ones from their lives before the Convent in the coda that closes the novel.

On National Identity, Self-Possession and *A Mercy*

Although the promise of intrafeminine coalitions is much narrower in *A Mercy*, Morrison depicts a multiracial community of women. In *A Mercy*, however, the narrative seems to show how cross-cultural identification is all but impossible because of the ways that colonialism—even without patriarchy—disrupts identification. *A Mercy*, like *Beloved*, examines slavery but treats race differently by representing free black characters and indentured white ones so as to highlight class differentiations and gendered disparities in the narrative. For example, although *A Mercy* takes place in a broad temporal space—the colonial period before North American colonies were united under the moniker "America"—that unified conceptualization of historical temporality moves through numerous locales that stretch down the east coast and across the Atlantic. The polyphonic narration in *A Mercy* is a means to investigate how women, Native Americans, and people of Afro-Caribbean descent are subjugated and destroyed by colonial power; the settings in which each of those categorical identities lives makes each individuated narrator part of a polyphonic protest against collective trauma.

By beginning with Florens' separation from her mother and moving through a series of reiterations of motherloss, Morrison seems to rescind the conclusions readers may have drawn in *Paradise*. Florens' subsequent inability to develop an attachment to a new maternal figure is indicative not just of her own psychic wounds but also of those visited upon untold millions of African American women and girls whose families were fractured by the slave trade in North America before abolition. The ways in which women's communities are disrupted by a nascent racial hierarchy in the New World upset any potential community the women may find together. As in *Beloved*, Morrison relies upon a forensic redrafting of history that the narrators must transmit textually with great verisimilitude to readers. This verisimilitude is achieved through meticulous research and integration of historical context into the writing—which is at once both fictional and quite true (in its representation of collective trauma), and allows the novel to generate a plausibility that may engross and persuade readers.

Of the three novels examined here, *A Mercy* is perhaps the best example of how historical detail can assist in the effectiveness of the historiographic function of testimonial fiction, when compared to the earlier texts. The novel explores the era in which African ancestry became firmly attached to slavery in the New World. White indentured servants express feelings of racial hostility and free black men have statuses that exceed those of white women. In *A Mercy*, Morrison seems to implicitly ask readers how the assumption of racial inferiority may have been taken for granted in the dominant historiography. Hence, the characterizations seem to encourage a deliberation about how that assumption may have been formed. For each of the female characters, the response to that assumption has everything to do with the buying and selling of bodies, labor and land that has led each of them to a particular place in a rigid hierarchy that even the absence of masculine authority cannot destabilize.

In a radio interview with Lynn Neary, Morrison points out that "[t]he notion was that there was a difference between black slaves and white slaves, but there wasn't" at the time in which the novel is set. *A Mercy* asks readers to consider what exactly initiates the racial ideology of American history. The readers, for instance, are asked to make sense of a terrible situation that causes Florens' mother to choose to give her daughter to a strange man, who will keep her in bondage, in the exposition and dénouement of the novel. This is, perhaps, not unlike the ways in which readers are asked to understand Sethe's decision to commit infanticide in *Beloved*. In spite of that point of overlap, the ways in which *Beloved* and *A Mercy* explore slavery are quite important. *A Mercy*, set in the 1680s, takes place before enslavement and African-descent were institutionalized as a set of unified signs—one signifier assuming the referent of both signs to make "slave" synonymous with "African American" as it is in *Beloved*. In an early section of *A Mercy*, one white indentured servant, Willard, complains to another, Scully, that the "natural" racial hierarchy of European above African, as they each perceive it, has been violated by the fact that they are enslaved while the blacksmith—a free man of African descent—is not. The racially motivated animosity is only ameliorated when the racial superiority of the white slaves is linguistically confirmed by the blacksmith using the deferential "Sir" to address the indentured white farmhand. Note that this utterance by the blacksmith to Will is the first moment in the text where the race of the farmhands is revealed to readers in transparent terms and it occurs 55 pages into the novel. Later, on page 67, Lina, a Native American servant to the Vaarks, refers to Will and Scully as "Europes," which seems to place them in the same category as the owner of the patroonship and to separate their status from the blacksmith's. Lina's view of whiteness as an emulsifying category is another way to complicate the color line depicted in its incipient moments in *A Mercy*. The withholding of racial signifiers is quite similar to the oblique symbolic maneuver Morrison accomplishes with the opening line of *Paradise*.

The withholding of race, either in sum or part of the novel, works in two important ways. First, the revelation of the indentured farmhands' whiteness may function to disrupt senses of solidarity by African American readers who have begun to identify with the characters because of the shared sense of historical trauma. In this way, the novel imaginatively produces a narrative absent from the dominant historical discourse. Second, the novel works to give voice to those enslaved during colonial times across three specific ethnic categories—African, European and Native American. *A Mercy* implicitly points to a historical void that Morrison's corpus has sought to fill, but one novel, or even all the novels Morrison writes about American slavery and its aftereffects, cannot plug the gap. Morrison's prose echoes within the largeness, and relative emptiness, of the historical space in which her narrative is set. She fashions her writing to seem "like entering into the Atlantic Ocean on a tiny little raft" because she could not give voice to the tens of millions of slaves whose perspectives are unrecorded. Instead, she seeks to enter "the minds and the bloodstream and the perception of individuals" within a "single narrative" (Neary n. pag.), which may have allowed her to also effectively inspire pathos in her readers, producing empathy through identification. This empathy may cause readers to examine the forensic testimony provided in the novel in an evaluative way that causes them to make judgments about the moral imperatives that emerge from the augmented history.

However, that empathy alone is not enough to guarantee the readers' awareness of the text's implicit information coalition building between marginal and outsider groups. Delayed revelations of racial difference also work as an instance of dis-identification for outsider readers who may have been tempted to ally their sentiments too closely with the African American characters. By exploring how indentured servitude during the colonial period comes to be understood as a racially-specific system of slavery, Morrison encourages readers to re-examine the ways in which they have come to understand the relationship between slavery and African Americans as well as between slavery and American literary traditions. Sophia Cantave notes that "at the turn into the twenty-first century ... modern readers want to bury the discourse under the fiction that 'we already know about slavery,' yet we do not know" (94). Morrison forces a confrontation with that which "we do not know" about the subject that we have willfully ignored, or been made to ignore. Further, she forces outsider readers to examine their own allegiances to characters and to be

especially attentive to differences in culturally determined identities that
are constructed around ethnicity and gender.

The merchant-class protestant perspective of Vaark's narration in the
second chapter reaffirms the content of Florens' disorienting discussion of
her mother's decision to give her way in the first chapter. In some ways,
Vaark's portion of the narrative works to help the reader retrospectively
make sense of Florens' portion of the story. In this way, a white male
character serves to authenticate the narrative produced by the slave girl,
which calls to mind a host of literary relationships between abolitionist
compilers and enslaved auto-ethnographers. Vaark serves as a secondhand
observer to the events that were so traumatic for her, and his observations
add to her credibility as a narrator when the reader may doubt her because
of Florens' obvious distress and confusion about the incidents she
describes. For instance, both Vaark and Florens characterize Senhor
Ortega as reprehensible. The low quality of life for slaves on Ortega's
plantation is set in stark contrast with Vaark's patroonship. The
slaveholder is a "papist" and an ostentatious fop who "turned profit into
useless baubles," and was "unembarrassed by sumptuary, silk stockings
and an overdressed wife, wasting candles in midday" (19). Vaark takes
exception to Ortega's Catholicism, even though he himself is not a
practicing Protestant.

The assumption of an evangelical Christian norm becomes more and
more firmly identified with Euro-American identity as the novel
progresses. Lina is sold into slavery by a group of Presbyterians; Sorrow,
the mixed-race servant Vaark brings back to the patroonship, is given
away by the first family that takes her in so that she cannot continue to
"distract" two Christian boys from their faith by being an available victim
for their rapacious impulses. Rebekka, Vaark's white wife, throws her lot
in with the neighboring community of Anabaptists when she takes ill. Just
as a racial hierarchy emerges in the novel, so does a religious one. There
are also class barriers that contribute to Vaark's hatred for the Portuguese
landowner. Ortega's spendthrift habits and inherited holdings in Angola
and Brazil serve as a counterpoint to Vaark's accumulation of property
and commodities through diligent labor. By creating such a contrast
between Vaark and Ortega, Morrison again invokes a trope of American
literature concerning slavery. For instance, Harriet Beecher Stowe
encourages readers of *Uncle Tom's Cabin* to consider how the differences
in the treatment of slaves at Arthur Shelby's farm, Augustine St. Clare's
plantations and Simon Legree's land shape Tom's fate, and in *Beloved*
readers are encouraged to make a similar comparison between Mr. Garner
and the schoolteacher at Sweet Home. In *A Mercy*, Morrison incites

readers to consider the events of the novel by way of evaluating the behavior of slaveholders. Like Stowe, Morrison disrupts the neat binary of slaveholders as either benevolent but misguided, or sadistic and self-serving; just as St. Clare's death prevents Tom from experiencing the freedom Eva begs from her father, Vaark's death will disrupt the "merciful" existence Florens' mother thought she could find for her child.

The titular mercy, which Morrison notes is a "human gesture" rather than any sort of divine absolution, is a mother's offering of her daughter to a stranger (Neary n. pag.). As Cathy Waegner notes, it is "[n]ot until the final chapter of the book" that readers see how this seemingly callous act can be construed as merciful (110). Only when "the mother recounts the horrors of the middle passage, slave labor on the sugar plantations of Barbados, and the sexual abuse on the tobacco plantation in Florida" can readers begin to understand "her willingness to put her daughter in the hands of a man who laughs rather than leers" (93). By withholding the rationale for Florens' nameless mother, whom she calls "minha mãe," to give her child to Vaark, Morrison implicitly invokes the painful context of slavery and its consequences for familial relationships. Literally "minha mãe" is Portuguese for "my mother," but Florens uses it as a proper noun or title, often preceded by an indefinite article. In using the novel to dramatize a white man's rescue of a black child from a dangerous situation from which a black woman cannot extricate her, Morrison redeploys that painful context within a familiar trope that reinforces some white supremacist notions. But to what end? And how can such a terrible, human "mercy" work to situate a cross-ethnic coalition between women?

Morrison's novel focuses upon the consequences for four women—Florens being only one of them—who are "unmastered" when Vaark dies (56). This is a significant maneuver that separates the most recent novel from its predecessors. In *Beloved*, Sethe struggles to find a way to be her "own best thing"—to understand that freedom gives her the ability to self-define in ways that are independent of the sum of her traumatic experiences. Likewise, in *Paradise* the women of both the Convent and Ruby are static—either mastered by the African American men who control the town or victimized by those same men in their passivity and stagnation. In *A Mercy*, masculine control and white supremacy are oddly not the largest prohibitive constraints on intrafeminine community. Gender, alongside race and class, becomes important for considering how colonialism and slavery function to generate oppressive institutions that are internalized. Because Rebekka, Lina, Sorrow and Florens are women "[n]one of them could inherit; none was attached a church or recorded in its books. Female and illegal, they would be interlopers, squatters ...

subject to purchase, hire, assault, abduction, exile ... They were orphans, each and all" (56–7). In the novel the similarly vulnerable positions of the women are presented in rapid succession to the reader, who must then grapple with the dissolution of their civil ties to one another. Morrison extends the ethnically produced solidarity among African Americans that is oriented on the historical trauma of slavery by positing a gendered dynamic for identification that permeates the racial boundaries that keep the women separate from one another. As Waegner puts it, the pre-Federal Maryland in which the novel is set presents a possibility for "cross-ethnic, cross-class coalition" (103), but instead of fictionalizing the realization of such a possibility, Morrison portrays "the subsequent opportune 'divide and rule' strategy of the colonial governmental and economic leaders" to demonstrate how that strategy produced a set of "new laws ... directed against the Africans, serving to link slavery firmly to blackness" (104) and, consequently, preventing women, who may work together as the women of the patroonship do, from moving beyond ethnic difference and into a gender-based coalition to demand equality.

Morrison alters dominant literary forms to re-represent the incipience of institutionalized racism that she argues produces a paradigm of American Africanism within U.S. national identity. Florens' narration is part confession and part coming-of-age story. However, "[u]nlike the traditional bildungsroman which shows the maturing subject being educated for a meaningful and productive place in the social fabric," Morrison's text illustrates how the interstitial pressures of patriarchy, white supremacy and class dominance prevent Florens from fully maturing (Waegner 94). She is caught in abjection resulting from motherloss, replaying the interrupted moment of separation from "minha mãe" at several instances in the novel. Florens sees "[a] minha mãe lean[ing] at the door holding her little boy's hand" when she worries that the blacksmith will not love her after he takes Malaik in. The fear of being replaced by the male child reiterates the schema of gender privilege to which Florens attributes her loss of her own mother, because her mother encourages Vaark to take Florens rather than her brother. Morrison provides the context necessary to explain the mother's reasons for seeing the risks to her daughter as greater than those to her son; in the final chapter, Florens' mother notes that "[n]either [Vaark nor Senhor] will want your brother," but Florens is not privy to her mother's reasons for choosing to give her away. Because of her ignorance of her mother's motives, Florens' abject status inhibits her ability to form a solid sense of self and this inhibition seems to have a causal relationship with her arrested coming of age in the novel. Waegner notes that "the modern female ethnic bildungsroman stresses the *creation* of the self-fulfilling social space by a marginalized figure who shows solidarity with the other disadvantaged women of her community" (101); however, Florens experiences no such solidarity. Motherloss contributes to the complexity and dysfunctionality of her relationships with Rebekka, Lina and Sorrow. Each of the female characters might have become surrogates for the lost mother, but the tensions that inhibit surrogacy are also caused by the intersections of categorical difference and privilege intrinsic to even the earliest versions of economically, racially and socially stratified American culture. Those stratifications do not always allow women to form bonds of solidarity across the differences they emphasize. Each of the women is subject to institutional oppression, but none refuse the small measure of privilege granted by their position above Florens in that hierarchy.

Rebekka, due to the shame and sorrow at the loss of her children with Vaark, would seem to be an especially apt choice of surrogate parent for Florens, as Rebekka might understand the girl's feelings of betrayal. Before her marriage, Rebekka was sold by her own parents and then shipped to North America, like any other sort of cargo, to a man she had never met. In a set of scenes that may present the only successful and functional community of women the novel contains, Rebekka makes friends on her transatlantic voyage. These women have socio-economic differences—one is an unmarried but impregnated woman, another is a thief sentenced to indentured servant hood, and the thief's mother and two others are prostitutes, marking them as lumpenproletariat members with even less status than Rebekka. In spite of those differences, their transitory status in the steerage hold and their shared sense of isolation and danger bring them into coalition. The shared experience of being treated contemptuously by the sailors, coupled with an intimacy that emerges from sharing their meager food and comfort together, creates solidarity. Onboard the ship they are not "[w]omen of and for men, in those moments they were neither" (80). No racial descriptors are attached to any of the women with whom Rebekka travels. Since the vignettes are filtered through Rebekka's narrative voice, the fact that no mention is made of race may indicate that the women were European. When living in the New World, Rebekka remarks upon the racial differences between herself and the women at the patroonship, so the absence of remark may indicate the ideological norming of whiteness. Alternatively, since the small airless space the women share is always pitch dark, perhaps the lack of visibility works to erase phenotypical difference—the women literally play in the dark. The absence of racial markers from the text may be another instance in which Morrison suspends that knowledge in order to prompt readers to consider how inter-ethnic communities might be theorized based upon these moments in the texts.

Rebekka's narration during the voyage calls to mind Morrison's first person narrative from the perspective of a newly enslaved child making the middle passage in *Beloved*. The women are crowded into a dark steerage hold, forced to sleep near their own defecation, berated by sailors who treat them like cargo rather than people, and deprived of adequate food and water. This has some echoes of the earlier novel. Likewise, the various reasons the women have for being forced to make the journey— either because they were sold away by their families or condemned and banished from their communities—may be similar in some ways to the situations that some Africans were delivered to their colonialist captors and shipped across the ocean, and they are situations also familiar to readers of *Paradise*. These are all points that may engender empathy across ethnically constructed boundaries. However, there are key moments where the differences in circumstance are made obvious. Beloved recalls the death of several of her fellow travelers, and how she remained confused and afraid for the duration of the journey. Rebekka and her compatriots use the voyage as an opportunity for temporary coalition building, which seems to allow them to avert the horrors to which Beloved bears witness. Their sharing of libations (which Beloved notes no one in her dark hold possessed) staves off the death by dehydration that the "man with the empty eyes" below Beloved suffers. Rebekka's camaraderie with the other women turns terror into humor when, in a sublimation of the threat of rape, they meet in the gaze of the sailors. One of the women confronts this threat but goes willingly to the captain's quarters—in part because she hopes for greater comfort and in part because she discovers that Rebekka is a virgin and will be rejected by her waiting husband if she is assaulted. It seems unlikely that this would have been a possibility for the enslaved women in *Beloved* if they had been threatened in the same way. These distinctions preserve difference while still dramatizing solidarity among different categorical identities.

There are reasons to explore the similarities in women's positions, regardless of those women's varied ethnic and economic identities, within *A Mercy*. Rebekka's status as an object that her parents sell to a stranger is echoed by the fact that the other women at the patroonship are all viewed as personal property, most to an even greater extent than the sold-away daughter they all call "Mistress." Lina is enslaved when her native community suffers a viral genocide; her home and family are decimated not by the direct, warlike tendencies of the "Europes," but as a result of a smallpox epidemic that seems to have been intentionally spread to her village by the colonists, gifting them with contaminated clothing and foodstuffs. Although she is "rescued" as a child from the pestilence by a group of Presbyterians, as a consequence she is physically and sexually abused by the pious man who takes her in. However, Lina never fully submits to this treatment and her refusal to patiently endure the violence of his racist and misogynist sentiments results in the Presbyterians' trading her to Vaark as a slave when she is fourteen. Lina's concern for the separation from her mother is textually intertwined with the loss of her culture. She has what Morrison terms "mother hunger," a pressing desire to both be and have a mother. Perhaps this desire is a mechanism for recovering the solidarity she enjoyed with her family and community before the small pox outbreak, but Lina, unlike Florens, seems able to draw a sense of self in spite of the motherloss she suffers.

Morrison explores the ways in which "mother hunger" may not be universal. Like Florens, Lina and Rebekka, Sorrow was abandoned and abused as a child. She is rescued from a situation much like the one that Vaark plucks Florens from, but Vaark's intervention is not quick enough to spare Sorrow from rape and impregnation by the sons of the first man to take the girl in. Sorrow's uncertain ethnic background causes Rebekka undue concern, and Sorrow's ignorance of her parentage and refusal to assist in the domestic work aggrieves Lina. Florens remains fascinated by Sorrow in the way preteens may often identify with young women, but the racial solidarity that Florens looks for in a replacement for her "minha mãe" is imagined rather than reciprocated by Sorrow.

Ironically, since the ambiguity of Sorrow's ethnic identity is at the crux of the other women's responses to her, Sorrow seems unconcerned about how ethnicity may function to identify her to others. The narration reveals she is unconcerned with forging relationships or attending to categorical differences. Her singular preoccupation is to find time alone to be with her imaginary friend, whom she calls "Twin," a capricious projection of herself with no clear racial or gendered markers. Sorrow, of all the women, seems the least caught in abjection because she identifies with no one. She ignores race, rejects the trappings of gender and repudiates motherhood. Never speaking of her own mother, only her father, the sea captain who disguised her as a boy, Sorrow initially shows no desire to either mother or be mothered. She refuses to actively consider her own pregnancy until after her child is born, and, of all the female characters in *A Mercy*, Sorrow is the least integrated into the women's community of the Vaark patroonship. She is childlike, and even when she delivers her child she treats it like a playmate—imagining that it is Twin—and does not participate in the women's never-ending labor to keep the house and farm running. Morrison uses Sorrow, the most liminal of the characters, to demonstrate the consequences of an extreme separation from community. Because of her ambiguous heritage, Sorrow might seem to be able to identify with all of the women—she might be Native, European and African. She, also, of all the women, bears the most visible mark of sexual exploitation—she is impregnated by her rapists and is unsure who fathered her child. This might be a mechanism for her to garner empathy from the other three, each of whom has either endured a sexual trauma or lived in fear of sexual assault. Alone among the women of the patroonship she is a mother, and each of them desperately envies her relationship with her child. Sorrow might have forged bonds with Rebekka, Lina and Florens by sharing in the mothering of that baby, but she refuses even that bond. In spite of all these potential avenues for relationships, Sorrow remains separate and alone, a kind of cautionary figure for those who would deny the possibility of coalition-building. Because all four women face the threat of sexual exploitation at the hands of men who are supposed to be stewards of their chastity and faith, Morrison exposes the common link between characters that could form solidarity through this shared trauma. However, the similarities of these instances of exploitation prove insufficient, which may be a metaphor for the outsider readers' attempts at identification and empathy across categorical differences. In creating and speaking through four female characters, Morrison is also able to disrupt the potentially hegemonic empathetic responses of outsider readers. The four women enact a hierarchy amongst themselves. Rebekka, as "Mistress" by virtue of her racial and marital status, tops this pecking-order. Lina, a Native woman who, in Vaark's narration, is figured as one of those "to whom it all belonged" because of the prior rights of tribal nations, stands next in this hierarchy, in part because of her longer history with Vaark than Rebekka can claim. Sorrow, whose ethnic heritage is indeterminate, claims the penultimate position, more by virtue of her age and status as an expectant mother than any systemically insured rights over Florens.

The ways in which one woman garners privilege only through domination of the others illustrates how the interstitial categories of identity that constrain those women are actively enforced through their claims to such a hierarchy. Readers who live within a system of ethnic privilege may do well to be reminded that "without the loose patriarchal structure of the patroonship 'family'" (which Vaark's masculine authority exercises over the women) the coalition they might form cannot hold. After her husband's death Rebekka will take up white privilege by "desperately adopt[ing] the prejudicial ways of the neighboring Anabaptist

community and begin[ning] to radically restrict ... free ethnic space"
within the household by curtailing Lina's traditional practices and
preparing to sell Florens (Waegner 97). In this way, Morrison examines
the issues of solidarity as an extratextual analogue to the problem the
narratives frame.

The narrative illustrates that hierarchy must be suspended, and
privilege relinquished, if connections across categorical boundaries to
constructed identities are to produce an affective alliance across
perceptually created and maintained color lines. Morrison's complex
structure works to place her didactic message in the bookending first-
person narratives of Florens and her mother. At the novel's close, "tua
mãe" (for the first time the woman becomes "your mother" in a direct
address to the child) tells Florens, in a narrative the girl child will never
hear, that "to be given dominion over another is a hard thing" (167). This
is a tentative condemnation of slavery, which seems to suggest that
dominion reveals the weakness of the person who possesses it. All four
characters living on the patroonship are damned in some way because of
the hardship of this gift. Rebekka's wasting disease seems to be the result
of her ministrations to Vaark, to whom she owed a kind of wifely fealty.
Sorrow's rejection of her child is a refusal to take the dominion over the
babe. Lina's loss of hope that she can mother Florens, and her
relinquishment of any sense of cultural continuity, seem to be a letting go
of her own self-determination. Florens' murder of the blacksmith when he
rejects her seems to be symptomatic of her will to "wrest dominion over
another," which in the mother's final narrative is described as "a wrong
thing" in a more strident condemnation. To be given dominion is difficult
but occasionally necessary, but to wrest it for one's self is wrong.
However, this final narrative also casts the giving of "dominion over
yourself to another" as "a wicked thing" (167), and this description is the
most condemning pronouncement the mother makes. Each woman gives
herself over in turn to either Vaark or one of the other women. The
difficult nexus of hard, wrong and wicked choices seems to mark the
taking of responsibility for privilege—if privilege can be understood as
"dominion over others"—and avoiding the wrong and wicked misuse of
that privilege. In exploring privilege in this way, Morrison asks readers, in
the voice of Florens' mother, to discover "alternate ways to be human
together" (Fryckholm) by sharing love and respecting freedom in
simultaneity. That sharing, in Morrison's novel, is the necessary
component for an ethical cross-cultural coalition.

A Mercy is organized around characters that have a preoccupation with
the intrinsic paradox of loving—which is portrayed as an intense

identification in all three novels—and being free—which necessarily mandates a separation from the other with whom one might identify. This preoccupation at the heart of the distinctions between Morrison's characterizations in the latest novel and the two that precede it may function as an apt metaphor for the sticky line between ethical and unethical reading practices for readers who engage with testimonial fiction. Just as love and freedom are entangled in a matrix of desire for the other and separation, so too is the outsider response to testimonial fiction. Readers outside the categorical solidarity of the group for whom the author speaks can either identify with the author and by extension that group. This identification would be to suspend the readers' subject position in order to render a judgment from the reader as if he or she was a part of the collectively identified group. Alternately, outsider readers can insist upon separateness that gives them the freedom to make a judgment about the novel from their own subject position. This double-bind cannot be neatly negotiated. For outsider readers and critics, the difference between approaching testimonial fiction through pure identification with the writer—a mechanism Wyatt has argued is more appropriately named "idealization"—or through a false-objectivist perspective that eradicates categorical difference and instead makes judgments from the outside, is fraught with tension. On the one hand, some amount of idealization of the writing subject is necessary for the historiographic function of testimonial fiction. This function is what allows one voice to become "representative of a larger class" (Nance 2) allowing testimonial fiction to link literary expression to social justice. However, in privileging a single narrative of systemic oppression, outsider readers collapse that larger class into the single narrative perspective with which they can identify.

On Testimonial Fiction and the Politics of Reading

Linda Craft notes that one of the most important features of the testimonial novel is that "it departs from the authoritarian narrative of the traditional novel as it experiments with discourse, form, technique and the status of the authorial subject" (26). Morrison's own expository prose also treats cultural context and readerly identification as effects of racial and gendered differentiation. In her essay "Rootedness: The Ancestor as Foundation," Morrison wrote that she "would prefer that [her books] were dismissed or embraced based on the success of their accomplishment within the culture" out of which she writes, rather than gauged upon "criteria from other paradigms" (342). This insistence upon relational contexts and categorical notions of collective identity may imply that isolating literary production from historical and authorial backgrounds is always doomed to repress parts of the text in ways that undermine interpretative endeavors that exist outside those concerns.

Morrison posits a series of concerns about how outsider readers can interpret and respond to the testimonial projects in *Beloved, Paradise* and *A Mercy*. The novels can be read as the literature of witness—they present an alternative account of moments of cultural trauma that shape American national identity. These testimonial revisions of history share some important features. Morrison dramatizes first-person accounts of trauma visited upon women's bodies. As Morrison's female African American characters present their stories, those characters, like their author, work to augment a dominant discourse about black womanhood for a mixed audience of readers. These characters' accounts also call readers' attention to the official histories their fictionalized accounts augment, and they implicitly call for deliberation on appropriate ways to memorialize and correct the atrocities to which the characters bear witness.

Unlike *Beloved* (which Morrison famously indicated was written with an audience of African American women in mind), *Paradise* and *A Mercy* examine intrafeminine communities that are not entirely African American. In crafting these casts of multicultural characters and examining their relationships, Morrison addresses both *Paradise* and *A Mercy* to this mixed audience in her representation of inter-ethnic communities of women; the novels speak both to African American women seeking their own places in American history and to an audience of outsiders who read over the shoulders of African American women. Morrison's address to that dual audience asks readers to confront the consequences of unethical interpretive practices and to consider their complicity in the systemic traumas visited upon the subjects of the fiction. Unfortunately, that transformation, no matter the quality of the narrative, is never guaranteed. Furthermore, the nature of any prediction about readers' perspectives is precarious; there is always a risk in testimonial fiction that the performance within the text may overwhelm the truth of the extratextual histories and experiences that the verisimilitude of the performance is predicated upon. Additionally, the subjective nature of readers' responses to every textual performance may indicate that singular truth, even unconstructed by fiction or narrative, is impossible or, at the very least, somwhat difficult to communicate across categorical differences in subject position. The risk of readerly misinterpretation of the testimony that the text delivers may, in some cases, mitigate the success of the transformative endeavor for the writer and the readers.

The relationship of reader to writer, of course, is shaped by the identity politics that the content of the novels seeks to investigate. In *Playing in the Dark*, Morrison argues that the context of American literature supersedes sub-generic or movement-based criteria because racial difference is so foundational to the American literary imagination. Concerns about authorial identity often overwhelm stylistic or periodic divisions. She argues that authors who are:

> [l]iving in a nation of people who *decided* that their world view would combine agendas for individual freedom *and* mechanisms for devastating racial oppression presents a singular landscape for a writer. When this world view is taken seriously as agency, the literature produced within and without it offers an unprecedented opportunity to comprehend the resilience and gravity, the inadequacy and the force of the imaginative act. (*Playing in the Dark* xiii)

The paradox of literature as an imaginative act that is both inadequate and forceful is perhaps what makes novels appropriate vehicles for the negotiation of identity politics within the system of cultural identification, particularly as that identification functions for a society that is paradoxically defined and constrained by a deep-seated anxiety about difference. According to Morrison, the racializing, and indeed racist, ideology of American literature can only be challenged through the self-representation of black writers and critics, who dedicate themselves to destabilizing America's myths about whiteness and neutrality. Morrison further indicates that African American writers, often like their African American readerships, have disparate approaches to, and expectations of, literary expression. There is as much variance within categories of identity as there may be between those categories. The varied approaches to African American women's testimonial fiction are shaped by constructions of racial identity in a uniquely American context.

Calls for solidarity through shared historical trauma become, in Morrison's fiction, a definitive boundary between outsider readers and the textual testimony. This explication of solidarity does not, however, account for differences within that ethnic category. Wyatt has argued that "the often unconscious desire to identify with, to *be*, the racialized other, produces a number of the misrecognitions that complicate race relations" (3). Whether ethical or not, some literary critics seem to suggest that identification through textual representation is a flawed vehicle for coalition building across ethnic and gendered categories. Indeed, Wyatt goes on to clarify the fact that "identification involves an assimilation of the other into the self and thus a violation of the other's autonomous subjectivity" (4), and this violation of autonomy not only risks the collapse of extra-categorical differences, but may also veil differences within racial categories. Wyatt, of course, is not alone in raising these concerns. Diana Fuss concurs, by claiming that considerations of outsider readers may even produce an "imperializing character" she sees as intrinsic to "many cross-cultural identifications" (8), and Doris Sommer goes so far as to claim that "identification is a murderous trope that reduces two to one" through the eclipsing of the alterity of the writing "minority" subject with the outsider reader. This kind of eclipsing is not usually the result of a hegemonic impulse or even a conscious desire on the part of the outsider reader to preserve his or her own ethnically-produced privilege. In fact, the eclipse often occurs because of empathetic responses that arise out of identification with textual representation, encouraged by the deliberative effect of the texts.

To achieve a better model for coalition building, processes by which in-group solidarity are formed might be adapted to generate more ethical sorts of identification across identity boundaries. However, such adaptations of this mechanism for generating solidarity must also work to minimize the risk that empathetic responses will overwhelm deliberation. If conversations about Morrison's novels from scholars across multiple disciplines and subject positions begin a process of knowing across ethnic, cultural, sexual and material difference, of creating solidarity without identification, then it seems a worthwhile pursuit to continue to engage in those conversations even when the coalitions produced by such scholarly discourse may be flawed.

Works Cited

Aguiar, Sarah Appleton. "Passing on Death: Stealing Life in Toni Morrison's *Paradise*." *African American Review* (2004). Web (accessed November 11, 2011).

Alcoff, Linda. "Who's Afraid of Identity Politics?" In *Reclaiming Identity: Realist Theory and the Predicament of Postmodernism*, eds. Paula M. L. Moya & Michael R. Hames-Garcia, 312–43. Berkeley: U of California P, 2000. Print.

Brown, Rosellen. "A Chorus of the Motherless." *The New Leader*, 30–31. November/December 2008. Print.

Cantave, Sophia. "Who Gets to Create the Lasting Image? The Problem of Black Representation in Uncle Tom's Cabin." In *Approaches to Teaching Stowe's* Uncle Tom's Cabin, eds. Elizabeth Ammons &

Susan Belasco, 93–103. New York: Modern Language Association of America, 2000. Print.

Darling, Marsha. "In the Realm of Responsibility: A Conversation with Toni Morrison." In *Conversations with Toni Morrison*, ed. Danielle Taylor-Guthrie, 246–255. Jackson: U of Mississippi Press, 1994.

Dawes, James. *That the World May Know: Bearing Witness to Atrocity.* Cambridge, MA: Harvard UP, 2008. Web. (accessed August 19, 2010).

Denard, Carolyn. C. (ed.). *Toni Morrison: Conversations.* Jackson, MI: U of Mississippi Press, 2008. Print.

du Cille, Ann. *Skin Trade.* Cambridge, MA: Harvard UP, 1996. Print.

Faery, Rebekka Blevins. *Cartographies of Desire: Captivity, Race and Sex in the Shaping of an American Nation.* Norman, OK: U of Oklahoma P, 1999. Print.

Franklin, Cynthia. *Writing Women's Communities: The Politics and Poetics of Contemporary Multi-Genre Anthologies.* Madison: U of Wisconsin P, 1997. Print.

Fryckholm, Amy. "Review of *A Mercy.*" *The Christian Century.* February 24, 2009. Web. (accessed October 9, 2010).

Gates, David. "Original Sins." *New York Times.* November 28, 2008. Web. (October 9, 2010).

Gates Jr., Henry Louis (ed.). *"Race," Writing and Difference.* Urbana, IL: U of Chicago P, 1986.

Gates, Henry Louis, Jr. & K. Anthony Appiah (eds.). *Toni Morrison: Critical Perspectives, Past and Present.* New York: Amistad. Print. 1993.

Heltzel, Ellen. "Toni Morrison's Powerful New Novel *A Mercy* Tracks, Examines Forces of Slavery." *The Seattle Times.* November 6, 2008. Web. (accessed October 9, 2010).

Hoofard, Jennifer. "Thinking about a Story: Interviewing Toni Morrison." *Writing on the Edge* 17 (2) (2007): 87–99. Web. (accessed January 6, 2011).

Elam, Diane. "Speak for Yourself." In *Who Can Speak? Authority and Critical Identity,* eds. Judith Roof & Robyn Wiegman, 231–238. Urbana, IL: U of Illinois P, 1995. Print.

Jordan, Don & Michael Walsh. *White Cargo: The Forgotten History of Britain's White Slaves in America.* New York: New York UP, 2008. Print.

Liscio, Lorraine. "Beloved's Narrative: Writing Mother's Milk." *Tulsa Studies in Women's Literature* 11 (1992): 31–46. Print.

Mantel, Hilary. "How Sorrow Became Complete." *The Guardian.* November 8, 2008. Web. (accessed October 9, 2010).

McKay, Nellie (ed.). *Critical Essays on Toni Morrison*. Boston: Hall, 1988. Print.

Michael, Magali Cornier. "Re-Imagining Agency: Toni Morrison's 'Paradise'." *African American Review* 36 (4) (2002): 643–661. Web. (accessed August 11, 2011).

Moore, Caroline. "Review of *A Mercy*." *The Telegraph*. November 13, 2008. Web. (accessed October 9 2010).

Morrison, Toni. *Beloved*. New York: Knopf, 1987. Print.

—. *A Mercy*. New York: Vintage, 2008. Print.

—. *Paradise*. New York: Knopf, 1997. Print.

—. *Playing in the Dark: Whiteness and the Literary Imagination*. Cambridge:
Harvard UP, 1992. Print.

—. "Rootedness: The Ancestor as Foundation." In *Black Women Writers, 1950–1980*, ed. Mari Evans, 339–45 New York: Doubleday, 1999. Print.

—. "Unspeakable Things Unspoken: The Afro American Presence in American Literature." The Tanner Lecture on Human Values, U of Michigan, 1988. Web. (accessed August 11, 2011).

Moyers, Bill. "A Conversation with Toni Morrison." *Conversations with Toni Morrison*. Ed. Danielle Taylor-Guthrie, 262–274. Jackson: U of Mississippi Press, 1994.

Nance, Kimberley. *Can Literature Promote Justice?* Nashville: Vanderbilt UP, 2006. Print.

Neary, Lynn. "An Interview with Toni Morrison for National Public Radio." October 8, 2008. Web. (accessed August 10, 2009).

Parker, Emma. "A New Hystery: History and Hysteria in Toni Morrison's *Beloved*." In *Twentieth Century Literature* (2001): n. pag. Web. (accessed January 1, 2010).

Ruas, Charles. "Toni Morrison Speaks." *Conversations with Toni Morrison*. Ed. Danielle Taylor-Guthrie, 93–118. Jackson: U of Mississippi Press, 1994.

Sommer, Doris. *Proceed with Caution When Engaged by Minority Writing in the Americas*. Cambridge, MA: Harvard UP, 1999. Print.

Spillers, Hortense J. "Mama's Baby, Papa's Maybe: An American Grammar Book." In *Feminisms: An Anthology of Literary Theory and Criticism*, eds. Robyn Warhol & Diane Price Herndl, 384–404. New Brunswick, NJ: Rutgers UP, 1997. Print.

—. "Cross-currents, Discontinuities: Black Women's Fiction." In *Conjuring: Black Women, Fiction and Literary Tradition*, eds.

Marjorie Prise & Hortense Spillers. Bloomington: Indiana UP, 1985. Print.

Teele, Elinor. "Untold History, Unheard Voices." *California Literary Review.* December 16, 2008. Web. (accessed October 9, 2010).

Todaro, Lenora. "Toni Morrison's *A Mercy*: Racism Creation Myth." *Village Voice.* November 18, 2008. Web. (accessed October 9, 2010).

Updike, John. "Dreamy Wilderness: Unmastered Women in Colonial Virginia [Review of Morrison's *A Mercy*]." *The New Yorker.* November 3, 2008. Web (accessed October 9, 2010).

Waegner, Cathy. "Ruthless Epic Footsteps: Shoes, Migrants and the Settlement of the Americas in Toni Morrison's *A Mercy*." In *Post-National Enquiries: Essays on Ethnic and Racial Border Crossings*, ed. Jopi Nyman, 91–112. London: Cambridge UP, 2009. Print.

Wyatt, Jean. *Risking Difference: Identification, Race and Community in Contemporary Fiction and Feminism.* Albany: SUNY Press, 2004. Print.

PART IV:

'IT WAS NOT A GRACE; IT WAS A MERCY': SPIRITUALITY IN THE AMERICAS

CHAPTER SEVEN

"MORE SINNED AGAINST THAN SINNING": REDEFINING SIN AND REDEMPTION IN *BELOVED* AND *A MERCY*

SHIRLEY A. STAVE

Readers of Toni Morrison's novels quickly discover that her texts engage in an interface with Christianity in a multiplicity of ways. Having chosen titles that reflect the Bible (*Song of Solomon*) and theological constructs (*Paradise*), and characters with names that spotlight biblical characters (Pilate, Shadrach), Morrison obviously intends her readers to ponder the significance of the West's dominant religion regarding her fictional creations. While many critics see Morrison's texts as in some way paying homage to, or at least growing out of, an endorsement of Christianity, I have consistently argued that I view her ongoing dialogue with Christianity as indicative of her misgivings with that religion, specifically insofar as the African-American community is concerned. On the one hand, Morrison never disparages the strength Christianity imparted to an oppressed group of people, nor does she belittle its significance during the Civil Rights years. On the other hand, Christianity provided the justification for chattel slavery and was habitually used as a palliative to encourage the oppressed to overlook their earthly suffering and to focus on a reward hereafter. Even more problematic, Christianity is not univocal. Over the centuries, various denominations have evolved alternative theologies and doctrines and, in many instances, practitioners of those denominations are fairly oblivious of the formal doctrine they claim to profess.

Reading *Beloved* and *A Mercy* with an awareness, as Eula Maddison claims in an article on *Beloved,* that "Morrison's [biblical] allusions are perhaps more than usually 'dialogical' in that often they function to problematize the very likeness they establish" (np) allows us to interrogate Morrison's understanding of the nature of sin and redemption. Not coincidentally, both novels construct an Edenic equivalent, which allows for an interrogation of the concept of innocence. In *Beloved*, Garner's plantation, Sweet Home, could be argued to represent slavery in its most benign form. None of Garner's slaves are beaten, all are encouraged to use their intelligence in resourceful problem solving, and food is plentiful and nutritious. Garner, the Creator God figure here, who was "tough enough and smart enough to *make and call* his own niggers men" (11, emphasis mine) and who "acted like the world was a toy he was supposed to have fun with" (139) [1] is revealed to be more innocent that his creations in that he lacks an understanding of human drives and human needs; while he may label his slaves "men," it becomes very obvious that he distinguishes between himself and them, seeing them as less evolved than he is. When Sethe asks Mrs. Garner permission to marry Halle, the white woman's first question—"Are you already expecting?"—is not one that would be ever appropriate to ask a white woman, and when Sethe asks if she will have a wedding, Mrs. Garner laughs and replies, "You are one sweet child" (26). Clearly, the slave owners do not assume their slaves are capable of moral or ethical actions, nor that rites of passage such as marriage might be of great consequence to them. Hence, for all of Mr. Garner's kindnesses to them, he infantilizes them, imposing his idealized expectations on them. Baby Suggs worries about his obliviousness to basic human needs: "Would he pick women for them or what did he think was going to happen when those boys ran smack into their nature?" (140). Morrison's critique of a God who lays down multiple injunctions regarding sexuality [2] that fly in the face of what it is to be human becomes apparent here. Additionally, a deity who is metaphorized as a father is predicated upon the continued child-status of his followers[3]. Slavery becomes the perfect metaphor, then, for the relationship between God as traditionally understood and humankind.

Garner's innocence is revealed to be lethal when, after his death, Schoolteacher takes over the plantation, wreaking unspeakable violence and devastation. Naively, Garner had never considered the future or the possibility of his demise and had never made arrangements for his "men." Aware that Sweet Home operated on completely different standards than the other Kentucky plantations, Garner nevertheless leaves his slaves to contend with the nightmare of slavery in its more typical guise, just as, many would point out, God appears oblivious to and helpless against the carnage that humans frequently must face. Baby Suggs, remembering the children that were sold away from her, claims "God take what He would," which would appear to be acquiescence in the face of God's authority, had she not continued "And He did, and He did, and He did" (23). Emily Greisinger questions whether Morrison is "commenting on the inadequacy of Christianity in the face of the profound evils of slavery" (690). While she concludes that Morrison is not, I disagree. The flaw in traditional Christian doctrine lies in defining God as both all-powerful and benevolent which, as philosophers have often pointed out, is inconsistent. The fact that tremendous human suffering continues to occur indicates a God so defined is either incapable of preventing it or heedless of the prayers of desolate followers.

Most of the discussion that has focused on the novel's intersection with Christianity concentrates on the character of Baby Suggs, who becomes a self-styled preacher to the ex-slave community of Cincinnati. Although Baby Suggs often delivers her sermons in the churches of various denominations and allows herself to be addressed as "holy," it is vital to interrogate her actual message insofar as it intersects with mainstream Christian theology. Morrison tells us: "[Baby Suggs] did not tell them to clean up their lives or to go and sin no more. She did not tell them they were the blessed of the earth, its inheriting meek or its glorybound pure." Rather, Baby Suggs insists: "in this here place, we flesh; flesh that weeps, laughs; flesh that dances on bare feet in grass. Love it. Love it hard … This is flesh I'm talking about here" (88). Carolyn Mitchell argues that Baby Suggs is preaching liberation theology, (35) a doctrine which indeed does require attention be paid to the physical needs of the oppressed. Mitchell elaborates: "Christ laid the foundation of a liberatory plan that must be activated and completed by us. This foundation is based on the interconnectedness of the spiritual and material, since our role as humans is to contain both spirit and flesh, and because we are bound by and to history as custodians of the earth" (28). However, liberation theology is extremely marginalized within Christianity and has virtually been denounced by the Vatican; fundamentalist Protestant groups have never accepted its premises as legitimately Christian. Emily Greisinger is more willing to grant the problematic nature of Baby Suggs' preaching, claiming: "Not *typically* Christian in its emphasis on the 'holiness' of the flesh, Baby Suggs' sermon is *genuinely* Christian nevertheless in understanding that salvation includes the body" (494). Appealing as Greisinger's claim is, Christian doctrine throughout history can be argued to have been antithetical to the body. Physicality has been viewed as tied primarily to the earth, rather than to heaven, and while various Christian creeds avow "the resurrection of the body," nevertheless human suffering in this sphere has most typically been regarded as inconsequential.

Helene Hinis acknowledges the chasm that divides the teachings of Baby Suggs from mainstream Christianity: "Contrary to the Gospel of John which claims that 'In the beginning was the Word, the Word was with God, and the Word was God,' Baby Suggs teaches the community that there can be no Word that excludes their physicality, no transcendental power or grace they cannot imagine here on earth" (187). Hinis maintains that "Baby Suggs preaches 'sanctification' as a state of ecstasy that is personal and simultaneously spiritual and physical," and that "this notion radically subverts established religious doctrines and church hierarchies" (187). It is noteworthy that nowhere in Baby Suggs' sermons do we find mention of a life after death. Rather, consistent with Morrison's treatment of the post-death experience in her other novels,[4] in *Beloved* the dead do indeed pass over to another realm, but they remain accessible and can return as spirits, even as flesh, in the case of the ghost-child. When Sethe is explaining to Denver how it is possible to "bump into a rememory that belongs to somebody else," the daughter states, "[T]hat must mean that nothing ever dies," to which her mother replies, "Nothing ever does" (36). Similarly, Paul D.'s route home from the slaughterhouse takes him "through a cemetery as old as sky, rife with the agitation of dead Miami no longer content to rest in the mounds that covered them" (155). Ella firmly insists to Stamp Paid: "You know as well as I do that people who die bad don't stay in the ground" (188), and none of the women of the community seriously doubts that the witch-child haunting Sethe is the embodiment of the child whose throat she had cut. This shared belief in the continuing existence on the earth of those who have died is incompatible with the Christian belief in a non-earthly life hereafter.

Pivotal to Baby Suggs' comprehension of salvation here and now is the necessity of community. As I have argued elsewhere,[5] Christianity is predicated upon the salvation of the individual; regardless of what clan or tribe or family affirm, an individual soul can break from them and be redeemed. By way of contrast, as Hinis points out, Baby Suggs' theology "constructs and affirms the ex-slave's identity in community and in history" (183). Colleen Carpenter Cullinan reminds us that the novel tells the "story of the suffering of an entire community of people" (82), all of whom are "as desperately in need of redemption as Sethe"(97). Baby Suggs loses her faith not because of anything God has or has not done; as we have seen, she does not seem to think God pays much mind to human misery. Rather, as Greisinger maintains, "*human* failure" (695) ultimately breaks her spirit. Never assuming even well-meaning white people can be relied upon, Baby Suggs is devastated when her own community turns against her, refusing to warn her of the approach of the slave hunters. However, as Mitchell points out, it is the community's "rigid orthodox interpretations of Scripture that shield them in their condemnation of Baby Suggs" (39). They justify their spitefulness by believing that "[l]oaves and fishes were His powers—they did not belong to an ex-slave who had probably never carried one hundred pounds to the scale, or picked okra with a baby on her back" (137).

Consistently throughout *Beloved*, the narrative voice insists that community is essential for human well-being. Sethe and Paul D. acknowledge their shame at their fond memories of Sweet Home, but, as Sethe insists, "But it's where we were … All together" (14). Being "all together" mitigates the awareness of their enslavement and allows for moments of fellowship and solace, a contrast to the devastating isolation experienced by the free Sethe and Denver. In Paul D.'s time on the chain-gang, he recalls how vital it was all of the men to be attuned to one another if any one of them were to survive. Their mutual dependence results in their understanding that "[a] man could risk his own life, but not his brother's" (109). Similarly, when the men are locked in underground cages during a flood, no deity intervenes to save a chosen few; rather the men must act as one: "The chain that held them would save all or none, and Hi Man was the Delivery" (110). While all serious readers of Morrison know how cautious she is in her celebration of human love, at the same time it becomes clear that she understands the salvific capacity of love. Hexed by Beloved, Paul D. finds himself unable to avoid his nightly encounters with her in the shed until Sethe's love breaks the spell. As she lovingly and playfully insists that Paul D. return to her bed, "The threads of malice creeping toward him from Beloved's side of the table were held harmless in the warmth of Sethe's smile" (131).

Salvation in *Beloved* in impeded not when humans separate themselves from God, but from each other. Sethe's murder of her child is not the act for which she is condemned; rather it is her pride in the aftermath of the event that antagonizes the community. Later, when Baby Suggs dies, Sethe further alienates the community by refusing to attend the funeral or to eat the food provided by them for the "setting-up." The narrative states: "Just about everybody in town was longing for Sethe to come on difficult times. Her outrageous claims, her self-sufficiency seemed to demand it" (171). Sethe's pride is predicated partly upon her lapse of memory. When she insists to Paul D. that "I got us all out. Without Halle too. Up till then it was the only thing I ever did on my own" (162), Sethe overlooks the significant role Amy Denver played in her survival. Without the runaway white girl to help her, both Sethe and the yet-unborn Denver would have died on the riverbank. Later, wounded by Paul D.'s abandonment of her, but thrilled to discover that Beloved is her dead child returned to her, Sethe foregoes the world and decides "Whatever is going on outside my door ain't for me. The world is in this room. This here's all there is and all there needs to be" (183).

Sethe's claim to self-reliance is revealed to be not merely short-sighted but lethal. Having lost her only source of income, Sethe and her daughters are on their way to starvation when Denver decides she must overcome her terror of strangers and seek help. Nevertheless, Denver is Sethe's daughter and thereby rejects Lady Jones' offer of assistance from a committee of church women, deciding that "asking for help from strangers was worse than hunger" (148). However, as Roxanne R. Reed points out, Sethe's "journey of spiritual healing and restoration" (56) is paralleled by that of the community as a whole, who must also overcome their mean-spiritedness and wounded pride. Hence, food begins to miraculously appear where Denver can find it and, in response, the girl seeks out her benefactors to thank them. It is this reciprocal relationship than enables salvation both of the body and of the spirit. Thus, whereas Greisinger argues that "Sethe must work out her own salvation by remembering and making peace with the past (689), I would argue that doing so is simply impossible. Without Denver and the community, Sethe would die from exhaustion and hunger, still locked in psychological conflict with her ghost-daughter. Cullinan is more on target when she claims that redemption begins with the women (99), but I would maintain it begins from the interaction of the women with Denver. As the women relate memories to the girl and delight in her shy words of thanks, they begin to feel compassion: "Maybe they were sorry for her. Or for Sethe. Maybe they were sorry for the years of their own disdain" (249). However, Denver understands that for them to act, she must demolish the wall Sethe had built between the house at 124 Bluestone Road by revealing the entire situation to them; she realizes, "It was a little thing to pay, but it seemed big to Denver. Nobody was going to help her unless she told it—told all of it" (253). As a result of Denver's disclosure, Ella, who was most set against Sethe, comes to realize her connection with the solitary woman, since Ella herself had chosen to take the life of a child she had borne after being repeatedly raped: "She had delivered, but would not nurse, a hairy white thing … It lived five days never making a sound" (259). Ella, however, feels no remorse for her decision to starve the child to death; rather, it is the "idea of that pup coming back to whip her" (259) that moves to her act. Nowhere does Christianity in any form figure in her actions. It is through her ability to sympathize with Sethe as a human being that Ella is able to coalesce the community to enact the exorcism.

The ritual that rids Sethe of the ghost child is not, I would argue, a Christian rite. Although the text tells us that the women who gather "brought what they could and what they believed would work. Stuffed in apron pockets, strung around their necks, lying in the space between their breasts. Others brought Christian faith—as shield and sword. Most brought a little of both" (257), Ella's response to the woman who asks if they should pray is telling: "Uh huh ... First. Then we got to get down to business" (257). It is clear that while Ella understands that prayer will not intervene in their actions, it is the women themselves who must "get down to business." Greisinger argues that the "syncretism of [Morrison's] method, the way she blends Christianity with black folklore, African tribal religion, and magic realism, does not significantly compromise her affirmation of Christianity" (700). I disagree. The novel makes clear that the outward form of the Christian Church becomes the vehicle through which the community, including Baby Suggs, practices a much older and fundamentally different form of spirituality. Cullinen states: "The redemption hinted at in this discourse of mothers is a redemption rooted in wholeness ... There is forgiveness implied in this embrace of all things, and healing, but the primary move is to gather all things together and speak of them as all part of the same whole" (91–92). Such forgiveness enables these women "to free themselves from the evil they had helped to create" (Cullinen, 98). No intermediary in the form of Jesus or his Mother appears in this discourse; rather the women themselves are the agents of the forgiveness and subsequent redemption; not merely of Sethe, but also of themselves collectively.

Cullinen's argument pivots upon the maternal discourse of the community, and while I completely concur that "the silencing of maternal voices is an enormous problem for theology" (78), such a woman-focused reading of the novel's theology does not take into account the roles played by both Paul D. and Stamp Paid (nor for that matter, Denver, who is not a mother but who is the catalyst for all the transformation that occurs at the end of the novel). Maddison reminds us that Stamp Paid's decision to forego his given name Joshua—a name, I would point out, overloaded with biblical significance—indicates that "he did not owe his salvation to the Lord; he was paid up in his own coin" (215). While Stamp Paid does "rely on the power of Jesus Christ to deal with things older, but not stronger, than He Himself was" (172), he also claims agency over his own actions in dealing with those with whom he interacts. His guilt at having revealed Sethe's past to Paul D. haunts him, and if the women of the community release Sethe from Beloved's spell, it is Stamp Paid who enables Paul D. to free himself from the bottle in which he finds solace. Again, it is Stamp Paid's decision to tell his own story about his wife, Vashti, who was forced into sexual slavery with the master, as well as his refusing to snap her neck for choosing life on those terms, that frees Paul D. from his despair. As for Paul D., the narrative voice tells us that there was "something blessed in his manner" (17) that encouraged women to divulge their innermost secrets to him. Again, the sharing of stories, the power of narration, enables salvation. Cullinen argues that for Paul D., suffering is primarily physical (83) and that although he does love Sethe, "his voice defines Sethe as something intensely other, something not even human" (83). I would argue, however, that Paul D. has long since overcome the physical suffering he experienced on the chain gang; what haunts him is the sense that his masculinity as well as his humanity have been compromised. Paul D.'s reminiscences about Mister, the rooster who stares at him when he is silenced by the bit, would be humorous were they not so devastating, since Morrison is clearly playing with the concept of the phallus or, specifically, the cock here. Even the rooster's name grants him a status forbidden to the slave. Paul D. tells Sethe: "Even if you cooked him you'd be cooking a rooster named Mister. But wasn't no way I'd ever be Paul D again, living or dead. Schoolteacher changed me" (72). Paul D.'s cruel remark to Sethe, "You got two feet, Sethe, nor four" (165), is driven by such anxieties. Paul D. knows he has had sexual intercourse with cattle, has been forced to perform fellatio on white prison guards, and has been unable to resist the sexual advances of Beloved who, having acquired the extent of her sexual education by watching turtles mate, forgoes the foreplay that turns human intercourse into more than merely a biological imperative and simply "hoisted her skirts and turned her head over her shoulder the way the turtles had" (116). We must also remember that although the women's ritual rids Sethe of the ghost child, it is Paul D. who saves her life. When he returns to her, she is quietly waiting for death as Baby Suggs had done, defeated by all that life had doled out to her. It is Paul D.'s desire to "put his story next to hers" (273), to share narratives that enable mutual salvation, that allows Sethe to perhaps accept her own self-worth and to choose life.

The exploration of the role of Christianity in human salvation touched upon in *Beloved* is brought far more sharply into focus in Morrison's 2008 novel, *A Mercy*. In her examination of the extensive biblical allusions in the latter work, Justine Tally maintains that "the sacred references are given a new interpretation, a rewriting of the Biblical model" (66–67). *A Mercy* is rife with multiple versions of Christianity, all of them at odds with one another. Morrison's critique is biting, astute and insightful as she interrogates the relationship of Christianity to various forms of domination, including racism, sexism and ecological irresponsibility. Although she puts the words in the mouth of her character Rebekka,

Morrison quite obviously concurs that religion is "a flame fueled by a wondrous hatred" (74).[6] To say that the author does not pull any punches is an understatement.

As she did in *Beloved*, Morrison here again premises an Edenic world, although she makes it obvious that the "sin" that destroys paradise is tied to Christianity itself. Set in the colony of Massachusetts in the late 1600s, the novel features a world lush with resources—"forests untouched since Noah, shorelines beautiful enough to bring tears, wild food for the taking" (12). However, the "Europes," as Lina calls them, do not arrive in an uninhabited land, but rather one that has been populated for centuries by a people who are capable of living in harmony with the land. Lina, who is indigenous to the "new world," remembers that "[h]er people had built sheltering cities for a thousand years and, except for the deathfeet of the Europes, might have built them for a thousand more" (54). Morrison's portrayal of the "Europes" makes it patently clear that it is their conception of Christianity that drives their viciousness and their destructiveness to each other and also to the land. Lina is aghast when Jacob cuts down an obscene number of trees ("without asking their permission" 44) to build a needless grand house that his ego goads him to construct. Jacob's ethos is derived, certainly in part, from a theology that he believes gives him dominion over the earth, that sets the physical in antithesis to the spiritual, and that sanctions greed. Consistently throughout the Hebrew Bible, Jahweh rewards his followers with the lands and goods of the peoples they conquer, and admonishes them to enslave or slaughter their former enemies. Although Jesus himself said nothing remotely similar and preached generosity, even while he condemned greed and the hoarding of wealth, Paul reinstated the understanding that owning land, goods and people is not inconsistent with a Christian life. Lina understands that the Europes "would forever fence land, ship whole trees to faraway countries, take any woman for quick pleasure, ruin soil, befoul sacred places and worship a dull, unimaginative god ... It was their destiny to chew up the world and spit out a horribleness that would destroy all primary peoples" (54).

Apart from perhaps the raping of women, none of the other acts she attributes to the Europes are actually prohibited by biblical doctrine. Christian doctrine would maintain that salvation for the indigenous people is available to them if they convert to Christianity, but doing so will not ease their suffering in the flesh. The kindly priest who teaches Florens to read baptizes her and her mother so that they "can have happiness when this life is done" (6), but can do nothing to affect their status as D'Ortega slaves, since even the New Testament condones slavery. When Florens' mother confesses to him the sexual depravity of both Senhor and Senhora D'Ortega, she reveals that "He did not understand or he did not believe. He told me … to pray for the deliverance that would be mine at judgment" (166). The Presbyterians who take Lina in after her people are eradicated by a smallpox epidemic are similarly kind to Lina, but their system of values is alien to her and, as Morrison scripts it, is revealed to be nonsensical: "[Lina] learned that bathing naked in the river was a sin; that plucking cherries from a tree burdened with them was theft; that … staring off into space to weep for a mother or a playmate was to court damnation [and that wearing] the skin of beasts offended God" (48). Even when Lena attempts to comply with such bizarre strictures she is nevertheless not permitted to participate in their religious services, and when she is beaten by her lover, who is one of them, they abandon her.

Morrison, however, goes even further in her critique of Christianity when she highlights the beliefs of Rebekka's parents, who are Dissenters of some sort and who neglect their children in their devotion to their God while they delight in ruthless violence against those whose religious practices differ from theirs. Rebekka's memories of "routine dismemberment" (76) are nightmarish, yet historically accurate. The viciousness that characterized the European religious wars between various factions of believers in the same God, never mind the witch burnings that were an attempt to eradicate older forms of worship, certainly gives credence to Rebekka's comment that religion is a "flame fueled by a wondrous hatred."

Initially, however, the novel suggests that Jacob, Rebekka and their extended "family" of servants might achieve a kind of salvation based on their mutual reliance on each other. Just as the community is required to cohere at the end of *Beloved* for the reciprocal physical and spiritual survival of all, so here, before Jacob's ostentatious proposal involving the house leads to death and dissolution, this group of raggedy orphans was thriving and relations among them were harmonious. Jacob and Rebekka work as hard as their servants do, and no one is treated cruelly. One can understand why the indentured servants Willard and Scully have idealized their situation as familial: "A good-hearted couple (parents), three female servants (sisters, say), and them helpful sons. Each member dependent on them, none cruel, all kind" (144). Were Jacob and Rebekka capable of viewing the situation similarly, the chances of this random community surviving Jacob's untimely death would have been enhanced. However, dependent as Jacob and Rebekka are on all of the members of their household, the couple refuses to acknowledge shared kinship with them. Jacob, who has inherited his land from a family member, believes his endeavors in the colony will allow him to achieve a kind of social superiority prohibited him in the more rigidly class-divided world of his birth. After his confrontation with Senhor D'Ortega, a member of the landed gentry, an exhilarated Jacob comes to believe "that only things, not bloodlines or character, separated them" (27). Similarly, Rebekka agrees to risk an ocean voyage to marry an unknown man partially because she is tired of "curtseying, curtseying, curtseying" (77). Neither of the two is willing to forego belief in their own supremacy.

Repeatedly throughout the novel, and throughout Morrison's entire ouvre, the greatest crime or sin a human can commit is the refusal to recognize a shared humanity with other humans, which is, of course, the impulse behind all systems of domination. As we have seen, the actions of the schoolteacher cause both Sethe and Paul D. to feel anxious that they might be not merely inferior in status, but actually biologically another species from their white masters. In *A Mercy*, however, Morrison locates that disavowal of fundamental affinity specifically within the overtly Christian characters. The witch hunters whom Florens inadvertently encounters commit their violations of her body in the name of Christ. Their perversity is not driven by fear that the child could actually harm them. Rather, their morbid curiosity originates from their regarding her as something other than human. Florens avers that they look at "me my body across distances without recognition" (113), and their doing so instigates Floren's "shrinking" and losing "[s]omething precious" (115). The text makes clear that Florens is not the only victim of their viciousness. They have masked their greed for the Widow Ealing's pasture in their self-righteousness and deliberately misread her daughter Jane's birth defect so as to permit their torture of her.

Morrison's sounding of the cacophony of disparate Christian groups in a world so sparsely populated would be amusing were the consequences not so dire. Catholics, Anabaptists, Quakers, Separatists, Presbyterians all populate the text and none can find any locus of correspondence with any other. Foregoing any concern with love or benevolence, they divide themselves on trivia, such as "the question of the Chosen versus the universal nature of salvation" (33). Morrison calls attention to their arrogance in claiming with no doubts that "Natives and Africans ... had access to grace but not to heaven" (99). Ironically, and sadly too, the Anabaptist women share with Rebekka their vision of heaven, which reveals their longing for the very physical pleasures they deny themselves even as they live. They long for "music and feasts; picnics and hayrides. Frolicking ... Skat[ing], even, on icy ponds with a crackling fire ashore to warm one's hands"(99). In this life, however, they shun happiness as

"Satan's allure, his tantalizing deceit" (97), embracing the very denial of the body that Baby Suggs' preaching so adamantly challenged.

The focus on an otherworldly salvation predicated on a rejection of the life in the body takes on specifically gendered terms here, as we repeatedly see that the men themselves do not practice what they preach nor what they impose upon all women. The Presbyterian man who beats Lina is not even reprimanded for his actions, while the Anabaptist deacon engages in sexual relations with Sorrow even as he comes courting the widowed Rebekka. What unites all of the women of the novel—mistress or slave, Christian or heathen, European or native, wife or prostitute—is the knowledge that they have no status in the eye of the law and that they must contend with "the promise and threat of men" (98). Rebekka has a moment of insight when she contemplates the biblical Job's indignation at God's refusal to respond to his suffering. Pondering her essential lack of existence, Rebekka thinks: "What shocked Job into humility and renewed fidelity was the message a female Job would have known and heard every minute of her life" (91). It becomes obvious that Morrison's sustained critique of Christianity in this novel is predicated not merely on that religion's abuse of the earth and its endorsement of slavery, but also on its debasement of women. Christ's brief attempt at disabling the gender hierarchy endorsed throughout the Old Testament is quickly undone by Paul, who once again renders women mute and invisible.

What separates *Beloved* from *A Mercy* most blatantly is the absence of a community in the latter work. Whereas the community initially fails Baby Suggs and Sethe, once they recognize their common humanity they come together to save themselves and Sethe. In *A Mercy*, however, no community coheres anywhere. Rather, we are given a sprinkling of co-religionists who gather together seemingly for the purpose of antagonizing those who do not share their beliefs. Modeled on the biblical patriarchal model, the European communities founded in the colonies are already doomed to dissention and violence from their inception. Having destroyed the indigenous culture that shared resources so that "everyone had anything and no one had everything" (60) and that honored "the majestic plan of life: when to vacate, to harvest, to burn, to hunt" (50), and replaced it with a system of entitlement for some and enslavement for others, the European colonizers instated an untenable way of life that cannot help but replicate the injustice of the system many of them were fleeing.

Additionally, Morrison makes clear that the "freedom" that would eventually be touted as the premise for the colonies becoming one nation is a vexed concept. While individuals may have desired freedom from religious or political oppression, they did not extend that freedom to others whom they regarded as erring. Hence, the witch hunters that Florens encounters have deluded themselves into believing they are just and pious when in plain fact they are vicious; in addition, while claiming to be concerned for the wellbeing of the community, in their actions they sow division. Repeatedly, we hear of illiterate indentured servants whose periods of servitude are extended by conniving masters who do not balk at cheating others out of years of their lives. And when Rebekka initially cannot be counted among the devout, her belief that "the satisfaction of having more and more was not greed, was not in the things themselves, but in the pleasure of the process" (97) is certainly shared by many of the European colonizers. What can salvation mean to a people so inherently corrupted?

As in *Beloved*, in *A Mercy* Morrison again perceives innocence as deadly rather than godly. Rebekka regards the Baptist women who are "convinced they were innocent and therefore free" as "[c]hildren ... without the joy or curiosity of a child" (92). Their idea of salvation, which of course can only exist in another plane, after death, is crude and narrow: "Other than themselves (and those of their kind who agreed) no one was saved. The possibility was open to most, however, except the children of Ham. In addition there were Papists and the tribes of Judah to whom redemption was denied along with a variety of others living willfully in error" (92). Yet it is to these narrow, severe people that Rebekka turns after recovering from smallpox. In attempting to achieve salvation on their terms, Rebekka effectively forecloses the possibility of the members of her household being able to thrive. Lina, Florens and Sorrow do not even have the status of legitimate widow. Morrison writes of them: "three unmastered women and an infant out here, alone, belonging to no one, became wild game for anyone. None of them could inherit; none was attached to a church or recorded in its books. Female and illegal, they would be interlopers, squatters, if they stayed on after Mistress died, subject to purchase, hire, assault, abduction, exile" (58). Essentially, the colonies have been established on the biblical patriarchal model, where men are accorded legitimacy and authority, and women only exist insofar as they are connected to a man through bloodlines or marriage.

Jacob and Rebekka's flaw stems from their misconception that they "[needed] no one outside their sufficiency (87). However, it becomes clear that that they do require, not God, but other humans with whom they can achieve what humans have always needed—community. Morrison places Florens' narrative of "shrinking" and feeling diminished near Sorrow's recognition that for Rebekka, "servants, however many, would not make a difference. Somehow their care and devotion did not matter to her" (130).

Rebekka refuses community because of her own sense of entitlement—as a European and the wife of a landowner; even as she judged the Baptist women for their narrowness, she partook of their value system. Hence, a devoted Native American woman, an African child she had doted upon, a half-witted woman of uncertain background, and two male indentured servants remain ultimately "other" from Rebekka—not human, not worthy, and certainly not entitled to the same privileges as she is, including, one would expect, the right to salvation. After all, she demands that Lina accompany her to church, but does not permit her to actually enter the building. She begins to beat Sorrow, requires Lina to forego her ancestral customs, and plans to sell Florens. But throughout her acts of cruelty, Rebekka believes she is eking out her own salvation. She no longer shares in the labors of those on whom she is dependent, but spends her time in prayer and Bible-reading. When she returns from church services, Florens says: "her eyes are nowhere and have no inside. Like the eyes of the women who examine me behind the closet door. Mistress' eyes only look out and what she is seeing is not to her liking" (159). Rebekka chooses to forego all joy and pleasure in existence in exchange for a hope of another life that would be filled with what she shuns here. Were her decision relevant only to her, one could pity the woman who has lost so very much, but the political significance of her act resonates throughout the lives of the other characters. As Morrison writes in *Paradise,* the people of Ruby have re-defined heaven as: "defined only by the absence of the unsaved, the unworthy and the strange" (306), and, more often than not, Christianity has operated from such a position.

At the end of *A Mercy*, Florens' mother speaks words that her daughter will never hear, words of wisdom that one might argue Morrison is passing on to her readers. Florens' mother trusted Jacob because he saw her daughter "as a human child, not pieces of eight" (166). In other words, he does not see "across distances without recognition," as the witch hunters, the Baptists, the Anabaptists, the Presbyterians and, ultimately, Rebekka see. As a result, Florens' mother places her faith in this very human man, who responds to her with pity and understanding, and removes the child from her precarious situation because "he knew there was no good place in the world for waifs and whelps other than the generosity of strangers" (32). As a result, Florens' mother claims his taking her daughter is "not a miracle. Bestowed by God. It [is] a mercy. Offered by a human" (167). Salvation, in Morrison's texts, reveals itself to be located in an earthly realm and depends upon the behavior of one human being to another. As long as a society predicates itself upon greed, entitlement, privilege, racism and sexism, salvation will remain an impossibility for all.

Notes

[1] Morrison, Toni. *Beloved.* New York: Alfred A. Knopf, Inc., 1987. All subsequent references to the novel will be from this edition.

[2] Admittedly, many of God's followers have made much more of sexuality than God did. While both the Hebrew Bible and the New Testament do lay down some prohibitions regarding sexual acts, in the Hebrew Bible they are included among dozens of other prohibitions concerning dress, grooming, property, work etc., most of which are ignored except by Orthodox and Hasidic Jews. In the New Testament, Jesus says very little about sexuality and a great deal about how lacking compassion and hoarding money will prohibit one from entering the Kingdom of Heaven, a message seemingly unheard by the same followers who endlessly carp about sins of a sexual nature.

[3] Eminent theologian Rosemary Radford Reuther maintains that such a paradigm results in "a kind of permanent parent-child relationship to God. God becomes a neurotic parent who does not want us to grow up. To become autonomous and responsible for our own lives is the gravest sin against God. Patriarchal theology uses the parent image for God to prolong spiritual infantilism as virtue and to make autonomy and assertion of free will a sin" (160).

[4] In *Love*, after her death, L. continues to observe the goings on of her community and, with Celestial, spends time by Cosey's grave. Christine and Heed continue their dialogue after one of the two has died. L. comments that May "thought death was going to heaven or hell. It never occurred to her it might be just more of the same" (135). In *Paradise*, the murdered women arrive on an island via a ship carrying both the "lost and saved" and we learn they will rest in the presence of the Mother Goddess "before shouldering the endless work they were created to do" (318) on earth.

[5] See my article, "Keri Hulme's Holy Family: Postcoloniality and Theology in The Bone People," *The Journal of Commonwealth and Postcolonial Studies* 17 (1) (2011): 20–39.

[6] Morrison, Toni. *A Mercy.* New York: Alfred A. Knopf, 2008. All subsequent references to the novel will be from this edition.

Works Cited

Cullinan, Colleen Carpenter. "A Maternal Discourse of Redemption: Speech and Suffering in Morrison's *Beloved.*" *Religion and Literature* 34 (2) (2002): 77–104.

Greisinger, Emily. "Why Baby Suggs, Holy, Quit Preaching the Word: Redemption and Holiness in Toni Morrison's *Beloved.*" *Christianity and Literature* 50 (2001): 689–702.

Hinis, Helene. "Re-Membering the Ex-Slave Self: Baby Suggs' 'Own Brand' of History in Toni Morrison's *Beloved*." In *Women, Creators of Culture*, eds. Ekaterini Georgoudaki & Domna Pastourmatzi, 181–90. Thessalonika: Hellenic Association of American Studies, 1997,

Maddison, Bula. "Liberation Story or Apocalypse: Reading Allusion and Bakhtin Theory in Toni Morrison's *Beloved*." *The Bible and Critical Theory* 3 (2007): 21.1–21.13. Online.

Mitchell, Carolyn. "'I Love to Tell the Story': Biblical Revisions in *Beloved*." *Religion and Literature* 23 (3) (1991): 27–42.

Morrison, Toni. *A Mercy*. Alfred A. Knopf, New York, 2008.

—. *Beloved*. Alfred A. Knopf, New York, 1987.

—. *Love*. Alfred A. Knopf, New York, 2003.

—. *Paradise*. Plume, New York, 1999,

Reed, Roxanne R. "The Restorative Power of Sound: A Case for Communal Catharsis in Toni Morrison's *Beloved*." *JFSR* 23 (1) (2007): 55–71.

Reuther, Rosemary Radford. "Sexism and God-Language." In *Weaving the Visions: New Patterns in Feminist Spirituality*, eds. Judith Plaskow & Carol P. Christ, 151–162. San Francisco: HarperSanFrancisco, 1989,

Stave, Shirley A. "Keri Hulme's Holy Family: Postcoloniality and Theology in *The Bone People*." *Journal of Commonwealth and Postcolonial Studies* 17 (1) (2011): 20–39.

Tally, Justine. "Contextualizing Toni Morrison's Ninth Novel: What Mercy? Why Now?" In *Toni Morrison's A Mercy: Critical Approaches*, ed. Shirley A. Stave & Justine Tally, 63–89. Newcastle upon Tyne: Cambridge Scholars Publishing, 2011.

PART V:

'THIS LAND IS OUR HOME . . .
BUT I AM EXILE HERE':
ALTERNATIVE GEOGRAPHIES

Chapter Eight

Post Racialism and its Discontents: The Pre-National Scene in Toni Morrison's *A Mercy*

Charles Tedder

In her 1992 review of Toni Morrison's *Playing in the Dark*, Wendy Steiner wrote that the author "is both a great novelist and the closest thing the country has to a national writer" (n.p.). This essay takes up the problems posed by a nonpolitical definition of nationality and the role writers play in creating or defining national identities through narrative. "The fact that [Morrison] speaks as a woman and a black," Steiner continues, "only enhances her ability to speak as an American, for the path to a common voice nowadays runs through the partisan" (n.p.). It might be helpful to remember that some African American writers have identified with a Black Nationalist movement, a nation within a nation, and that they do not, it is safe to say, see a common voice on the other side of the partisan. Notwithstanding Morrison's well-known rejoinder to the question of how to label her writing—that no one complains that Joyce wrote about the Irish—her novels have by and large been understood as representing and speaking to a specific subset of Americans, a fact made clearer by the extent to which her 2008 novel *A Mercy* follows from the critical assertions of *Playing in the Dark* and more explicitly represents many American nationalities. Her best-known work, *Beloved*, confronts the cultural legacy of slavery through particular characters who survived and remember the days before abolition. In contrast to that novel's specificity, *A Mercy* expands the scope of cultural memory work and articulates a national origin story for a post-racial America. Whereas *Beloved* represents the processing of traumatic memory in the precise experience of African Americans, their families and communities, *A Mercy* takes on the traumatic past as a problem for communication and cooperation across lines of descent—a problem that resonates in the so-called post racial sociopolitical context of early twenty-first century America.

In a time when we tend to conflate the concepts of nation and nation-state, it will help to designate a precise definition of nationality. According to John Stuart Mill's 1861 *Considerations on Representative Government*, "A portion of mankind may be said to constitute a Nationality, if they are united among themselves by common sympathies, which do not exist between them and any others" (n.p.). This solidarity can be bounded in many ways, including the use of designations of "race and descent," "language" or "religion." While many of these are common to the characters in *Beloved*, none of them are fully shared by all the characters in *A Mercy*. "But the strongest of all," Mill tells us, "is identity of political antecedents; the possession of a national history, and consequent community of recollections; collective pride and humiliation, pleasure and regret, connected with the same incidents in the past" (n.p.). In the former novel, Sethe and Paul D. have in common a lived experience of slavery, which is indirectly shared by others who were not themselves enslaved. In the latter, there is no such common history that unites the members of the story's small community. In this way, the scene is set for a narrative meditation on what is, more broadly speaking, the principle problem for the discourse of community in American fiction—whether the United States is a "multicultural" or a "multinational" society. *A Mercy* is set circa 1690, a time not only before the fullest expansion of chattel slavery in the South, but also before the creation of the United States government. By recollecting this originary period, the novel may question to what extent all Americans can have a "connect[ion] with the same incidents in the past" that can sustain, in Mill's terminology, the necessary "fellow-feeling" sufficient for a representative government (n.p.). By his reckoning, "free institutions are next to impossible in a country made up of different nationalities" because if the people do not share a national identity, then "the same incidents, the same acts, the same system of government, affect them in different ways; and each fears more injury to itself from the other nationalities, than from the common arbiter, the State" (n.p.). In this way, the government would tend towards despotism because its factions would be unable to cooperatively maintain the freedom of their institutions.

If we follow Mill's argument a little further, to the extent that ethnicity has come to stand in place of nationality, we might believe that only a post-ethnic American political identity could support a truly progressive, liberal government. It is worth noting that *A Mercy* saw publication the same year as the election of the first black president of the United States—

in fact, Barack Obama became the first non-white leader of a majority white country. His campaign occasioned no little reflection on America's past, but this was not always affirmative or productive. When Michele Obama commented that she was proud of her country for the first time, she was roundly criticized for feeling otherwise before. That reaction illustrates the lack of a common national history—or at least, a common understanding of the nation's history.

Nations and Ethnicities

Nationality, in Mill's sense of the word, depends on not only a common set of experiences but also a consensus about the meaning of historical events. Accordingly, those who publically remember and interpret the past have a special leverage in defining national identity. In late twentieth-century American fiction, more than one author has fictionalized history in order to create a sense of identity that survives (to live beyond) the traumas of the past. In her 1995 article "Surviving What Haunts You," Naomi Rand discusses Toni Morrison, Philip Roth and Leslie Marmon Silko. Spelling out the tension between claiming a group history and establishing an individual identity, Rand explains that "with an acknowledgment of a particular cultural heritage comes a delineation, an enforcement of individuation which is finally at odds with the desire for homogeneity and acceptance that might be called on of the basic American myths" (21). Morrison and other writers "must struggle with their pasts as with their demons" partly because they are haunted by "the vision of a truly 'New World' where past and present are unable to coexist amiably" (22). This persistent, haunting past is reflected in the use of narrated memories that indicate the "still ongoing battle between possible and impossible versions of the world" (30). Ghosts in particular "serve as a link between the visible and invisible, between guilt and freedom from guilt" that ultimately forbids any forgetting of the past (31). Rand underlines this point when she observes that:

> As Americans, we are taught that we can free ourselves, can cut the ties that bind us to the past, but the line between the visible and the invisible is not as tenuous as we would like to believe. For Morrison, Roth, and Silko, the act of separation must entail resuscitation, and even a resurrection, perhaps because those who do not study history are condemned to repeat it. (31)

This final platitude indicates the horizon of Rand's argument at the time. Severing oppressed people from their roots in a differential identity that can be an important source of strength is a well-known instrument of systemic domination. But resistive historical fiction is more complicated than a mere imperative to never forget. There is a particular kind of active memory—what Morrison refers to as "rememory"—a re-thinking (re-cognition) of the past as not the history of *either* the dominating *or* the dominated, but rather as the shared history of both. In *A Mercy*, Morrison not only speaks to what haunts African Americans and Native Americans separately, but also what haunts these groups and Anglo Americans collectively, albeit differentially.

Invoking the past to inform present behavior affects not only "ethnic" writers, but also ostensibly non-ethnic writers. The call to remember the American dead—usually with no acknowledgment of diversity among the dead, and hence a de-ethicizing or whitening of them—continues to be the principle lever of patriotic quietism. Criticisms of the American social order can and often have been silenced by the accusation of disloyalty to the nation-state because they disrespect what so many have died for. This invocation of the fallen soldier consolidates national identity through a process that Benedict Anderson calls the "reassurance of fratricide." Anderson explains, convincingly, that when nationalists tell the history of a singular group consciousness "awakening" as if from sleep, they frequently employ a trope of "speaking for the dead," by which they can, "with poignant authority, say what [the dead] 'really' meant and 'really' wanted" (198). What the ventriloquized dead wanted, it comes as no surprise, was to succeed at supreme personal sacrifice in founding the "awakened" nation, whichever one it may be. Thus uncritical love and blind duty are a blood debt owed to the dead, to the fixed narrative that they died for. This kind of myth creates the impression of a monologically binding and hence national sequence that demands one's loyalty to the status quo. The anti-revolutionary uses of such teleology are clear—when certain conditions are assumed to be inevitable, any resistance to those conditions seems impossible or unwise.

However, the narrative of the dead need not always be a nationally-binding or ethnically-expunged narrative, a story of the death of faceless individuals in service to the birth of a nation (to use a loaded phrase). Writers of fictions can compose alternative mythologies, even anti-mythologies. The motivation and consequence of telling these kinds of stories must be an alternation to our understanding of identity and community. That is, if the function of national history is to provide a national identity, then whatever change to our understanding of that history must also change our sense of what it means to be, in this case, American. Morrison avoids the usual ventriloquism of the nation's dead by imagining a past in which the dead did not in fact give their lives for the sake of the present status quo. The characters in *A Mercy* cannot have done so because they could not have agreed among themselves, in their diversity, on what their future (our present) should be, if they thought of us at all (and in the novel, they don't). We cannot be cajoled by our debt to their sacrifice if they did not make that sacrifice for the sake of a great work to which we are now beholden.

Whether deliberate propaganda, racist pseudoscience, or the "genuine" elements of cultural traditions, origin stories usually explain the creation of people like the ones telling and hearing them, although many include, as an episode in the myth cycle, a first tribe's division into the various peoples scattered about the earth. Novelists who imagine alternative origins, whether mythical or historical, are not only writing one story over and against another. By choosing how to imagine and narrate the past, they structurally communicate a set of ideas about human freedom and agency. A teleological framework will represent the past as either (1) a mythical narrative that explains the present, or (2) a historicist dialectic that inevitably leads to the present. In this second case, the historicist tends to assume that because the past has produced the present, it *must* have done so. This paradigm reifies the present as the *inevitable* result of the past. We tend to feel this in our everyday lives; for example, if we think our parents' union inevitably produced ourselves, ignoring the countless other individuals that could have been born in our stead. Up until very recently, these myths and histories have been routinely particular and ethnocentric—creation is the story of how *our* people came to be; history is the story of *our* nation struggling to be born. In either case, there is a tendency to see the coming into being of the present world only in terms of a particular kind of human being. This singular inhabitant goes along with the assumption that the present is the natural product of the past, whether the means of production is the magical will of a narrating god or the material dialectic of a history. In opposition to the ethnically bound world of the foregoing ontology, *A Mercy* presents the process of becoming-present as a work of contingency and coincidence, and so pictures a world that always has been and always will be occupied by many kinds of mutually 'othered' peoples.

The past-future axis of narrated history interacts with a perpendicular spectrum of identity groups, whether these are understood as nations or ethnicities. Mill specifies that something like ethnicity—a shared race or culture—may be the grounds for national solidarity. A national identity that includes multiple ethnicities must perforce have a stronger hold on the loyalties of those who belong to it than their ethnic identities do—at least, in the normative version of the post-ethnic assertion. When this is not the case, there arise nations within nations, such as the Black Nationalists, identifiable nationals living within the jurisdiction of a state with whose nation they do not identify. There is also an empirical form of the post-ethnic claim—the existence or importance of one kind of human relationship has weakened in the twentieth- century in favor of another. Werner Sollors's *Beyond Ethnicity* (1986) establishes conventional terms for the types of relationships involved, such as "consent" versus "descent":

> Descent relations are those defined by anthologists as relations of "substance" (blood or nature); consent relations describe those of "law" or "marriage." Descent language emphasizes our positions as heirs, our hereditary qualities, liabilities, and entitlements; consent language stresses our abilities as mature free agents and "architects of our fates" to choose our spouses, our destinies, and our political systems. (6)

In this passage, the past-orientation of descent clearly contrasts with the future-orientation of consent, and it follows that descent language tends toward the ideological maintenance of the status quo, while consent language holds the promise of something new and other than what the past demands. When Anderson observes the rhetorical power of the ventriloquized dead in forming national identity, he is describing a kind of descent relationship; one that limits the freedom of today's individual by demanding a renewal of the projects for which his or her forebears have died. Consent relations, *ipso facto*, are defined by an active individual choice that only obtains with the possibility that we today are not required to take up the projects of our ancestors.

Without doubt, the existential freedom of the subject-agent in the consensual scheme of things has been overstated—people may be able to choose their affiliations, but those choices are always shaped, informed and limited by material circumstances which exist as effects of past causes. A tendency to play up consent over descent does not mean that the past is utterly cast off, only that its grip is loosened somewhat. How much loosening is really helpful is an argument that won't be settled here. Caroline Rody, for example, finds the post-ethnic school to be blind to the felt, lived experience of inherited identity; she prefers the term "interethnic" (10–11). And, certainly, we may sometimes choose solidarity within an essentialized group identity for strategic, political reasons. Ethnic identities are not only descent relationships that may make freedom-limiting demands on individuals. They paradoxically allow for a sense of self by endowing a sense of group belonging, and consent relations depend upon a people making choices for themselves. Stuart Hall eloquently describes the necessity of ethnic identity in the following passage:

> There is no way, it seems to me, in which people of the world can act, can speak, can create, can come in from the margins and talk, can begin to reflect on their own experience unless they come from some place, they come from some history, they inherit some cultural traditions. What we've learned about the theory of enunciation is that there's no enunciation without positionality. You have to position yourself somewhere in order to say anything at all. Thus, we cannot do without that sense of our own positioning that is connoted by the term ethnicity. (18)

For Hall, positionality is not a monolith, a one-place inherently assigned or occupied by one group, tribe or ethnicity. It is a necessary condition for individuals to exercise some intentionality over their own processes of becoming. To take away that condition is to limit individuals to being this-or-that and having no materials with which to compose their own understanding of history. Sollors acknowledges this limit of post ethnicity when he writes that "Somebody's claim to universalism may easily become somebody else's restriction to particularism, as long as an ideal is identified not with total human striving but with a place on the map or a secular interest" (260). The problem with getting a sense of "total human striving" has, of course, been complicated by the fact that most human striving is against other humans.

The difficulties that confront post racial American politics today—which is also the problem of post ethnic or post cultural American identity—is that the shared past is so very, painfully different for distinct identity groups. The work of *A Mercy*, it seems to me, is to confront whether that past can be understood in a way that honors differential histories while also uniting the various inheritors of those histories today. The novel explores, in Hall's terms, the becoming rather than the being of American national identity—the possibility of what he calls "emergent ethnicities [that have] a relationship to the past, but it is a relationship that is partly through memory, partly through narrative, one that has to be recovered" (19). *A Mercy* asks its readers to contemplate just such a relationship to the past, a mixture of descent and consent, of cultural recovery and invention.

Piecing Together a Past

Morrison's fictions are not only stories often set in the past, but also narrative depictions of individuals performing recollection. Very often, characters recreate these personal pasts in dialog with pastoral or Arcadian tropes. Caroline Rhodes points to the Sweet Home plantation in *Beloved* as one such utopia. I could submit, also, the ex-slave's farmstead "Lincoln's Heaven" in *Song of Solomon*. Both are sites of nostalgia and longing but also pain that must be absorbed by the protagonists. Narrated processes of recovery in *Beloved* may be read as metonyms for African American community as a whole (at least, this is one usual reading). Morrison's later work *Paradise* exhibits the interweaving of narratives that Rhodes identifies with the "disorienting, disjointed function[ing]" of memory. But in this case, two intentional communities—one African American, and the other a kind of women's shelter—are formed side-by-side and put into tension with each other, with the differences created between generational experiences of different forms of oppression. For the oppressed, the task of achieving the good life cannot not be imagined as the struggle in and against a historical backdrop. It follows, then, that success would usually and reasonably be imagined as the fulfillment of a historical progress. Giving up teleology is as much a problem for progressivism as it is for conservatism. The theory of history embodied in narrative structure becomes the vehicle for what a story can say about our relationship to the past and each other.

A Mercy is therefore not a speculative history in the science fiction style of Henry Turtledove or Philip K. Dick. Nor is it, strictly speaking, an inventive re-take on historical events, as is Charles Johnson's *Dreamer*, or a historical fantasy such as Octavia Butler's *Kindred*. These novels are related, of course, if by no other kinship than the fact that Morrison, Johnson and Butler all take up the history of African American identity. Yet *A Mercy* is distinguished from these in a way that *Beloved* is not, insofar as its performance and representation of "rememory" goes beyond the boundaries of any one ethnicity. The novel shows that forging an identity out of the past is not a conservative act of not forgetting history, but rather a progressive process of reinterpreting cultural memories. If one can, in fact, reinterpret or rewrite personal histories as needed, then likewise present identity positions become, in a new partial sense, consensual. An intentional and mindful connection to the past can open up possibilities for post racial politics while, in Morrison's words, maintaining the imperative to "walk that line" because "you don't want the culture de-raced" (Rustin, n.p.). In another sense, insofar as the individual has the power to actively interpret the past, "rememory" offers a way of thinking about history that does not generate a sense of inevitability or destiny.

It may be sufficient to define "rememory" as reinterpreting memory, but a supplemental description underlines its liberating power. Jewell Parker Rhodes defines the process of "rememory" as "a way of finding your bearings in a historical context." Her comparison of memory and "rememory" is a particularly insightful:

> Memory is a disorienting, disjointed function which Morrison captures through the complex layering and interweaving of her narrative structure. The process of memory itself becomes an event as states of mind provide for the incremental catharsis of the self. Rememory, on the other hand, is a revisionary process of memory, of seeing things for what they were, not for what you thought them to be at the time, of seeing things again in the light of present circumstances, and of weighing the value of past events in order to build a foundation for living in the present and the past simultaneously. (77)

Written to comment on *Beloved*, this description does not fully account for the shift from the individual to the communal that Morrison's work repeatedly performs. Rhodes reads *Beloved* (partly) as the story of how Sethe comes to terms with her memories of the Sweet Home plantation as a bitter place, a plantation dystopia rather than a pastoral utopia, "seeing things for what they were" (77). However, this appeal to the actual, real or matter-of-fact truth of the past does not function very far beyond the limits of an individual's living memory. Rhodes emphasizes the "incremental" and "foundational" memory-"rememory" processes of a particular self. Moreover, this self must be cleansed (undergo catharsis) in order to become clear-sighted. While, again, this works well as far as it goes in *Beloved*, it does not address concerns with what cannot be the sole domain of any individual memory or what has not been retained in personal memory at all, which are the contexts for *A Mercy*. There remains the issue of the past that is "lost" or unrecorded in personal memory or the historical record, and it is this past that most urgently needs to be imaginatively reconstructed. The acts of community that one individual might extend to others, generously, is precisely what Morrison points us toward in *A Mercy*, foremost in the title itself.

Set almost century before the Declaration of Independence, *A Mercy* reimagines nascent America through a *dramatis personae* that illustrates identity as a matrix of different affiliations. Thus in its timing (mythic colonial past) and spacing (the diversity of characters), the story stages "rememory" on a grander scale than the author's previous novels but in a way already anticipated in her critical writing. In *Playing in the Dark*, Morrison contests the colonial casting of American identity in the image of a new white man. In *A Mercy*, she contrasts that white man, in the character of Jacob, not only with an Africanist presence in the characters of Florens, Florens' mother, and the Blacksmith, but also the presences of women, American Indians, homosexuals, the mentally disturbed, the poor and the indentured. In *Paradise* the best of all possible worlds cannot be successful only in terms of being black or being a woman, and in *A Mercy* it cannot be imagined in terms of any single identity drawn according to any of several positionalities.

The community space of *A Mercy* is a farmstead belonging to Jacob, a merchant and "American Adam" who is both central and peripheral to the novel. He is central as the owner of the farm and some of its inhabitants—they are connected to each other initially through their relationship to him—but also peripheral because he is dead for most of the narrative. This reinterpretation of the colonial scene undoes the call of the patriotic dead because neither Jacob nor any of the farm's other inhabitants see themselves as the founders of a new nation in the *tabula rasa* of a new world. Jacob is dissatisfied and ornery, especially unhappy about the differences of religious affiliations between various fiefdoms. Jacob's wife Rebekka made the Atlantic crossing out the economic necessity of an arranged marriage. His servant Lina is an American Indian whose village was decimated by smallpox; she is christened "Messilina" by "kindly Presbyterians," who teach her that her traditional behaviors are wicked before they give up on her conversion. The mentally disturbed Sorrow is shipwrecked as a young girl and adopted by a local sawyer; later, she is raped and impregnated by his sons. Jacob accepts the slave Florens in trade for debts from a Maryland squire, motivated partly out of compassion based on his own past as an orphan and partly by a sudden ambition to become a prosperous plantation owner. It is this transfer of Florens, from her mother to Jacob, that forms the main conflict of the story—throughout her narration, Florens wrestles with the pain of having been given away by her mother. One and all, the members of this community arrive at the farm through choices not their own. Even the two politically free characters, Jacob and the Blacksmith, have personal histories of transatlantic displacement. There are no bonds of "descent" such as by blood or inheritance, and to call the bonds of law that unite most of these characters in patriarchal marriage, slavery or servitude to Jacob a kind of "consent" would be cruel at best. This community exists and cannot be adequately described by either category of relationship. Most importantly, none of the characters, not even Jacob, are the ideal "new white man," creating a brave new "land of the free."

Primal Scenes

On the first page of the novel, as Florens begins her telling, we read "I see a minha mãe standing hand in hand with her little boy" (3). The minha mãe, Portuguese for "my mother," is an after-image or echo of Florens' mother. The girl is haunted by her mother's choice, by the choices of another person that have shaped her life. Her distress is not unlike Beloved's "clamour for a kiss." The giving of Florens qualifies in Ashraf Rushdy's account of "rememory" as a "primal scene" that the narrator is compelled to remember at crucial moments in order to resolve a crisis. In his discussion of *Beloved*, Rushdy describes several specific scenes in the novel: Sethe and Paul D. both must confront their past experiences on the Sweet Home plantation. This is an intra-cultural past, something that the characters confront together as ex-slaves. Then there are Sethe's own intrapersonal primal scenes, including the day she was raped and the day she murdered her child. In Rushdy's analysis, Sethe and Paul D. are able to unify their separate, scattered memories into a set of interdependent stories, such that each "discrete primal scene become[s] a sequence in a unified narrative" (318–19). The interdependence of the stories in *Beloved* is similar to the interweaving of narratives in *A Mercy*. However, in the later novel, the process of cooperative "rememory" concerns not only those who share a particular experience of the past (e.g. as ex-slaves), but rather all those individuals who are present in a given time and place. It is a set of relationships defined by proximity rather than nationality, consent or descent.

There are many primal scenes in *Beloved,* but one stands out from the others for its pain and consequences—Sethe's act of infanticide . It would not be incorrect to say that the day when Florens is given to Jacob is the parallel case in *A Mercy*. In both novels, a mother does something cruel to her child in the belief that it is more merciful than the alternative—that child's degradation and the hands of a white man. There are structural indications that this is the central scene in *A Mercy*—the chapters alternate between Florens' closely narrated experiences in pursuit of the Blacksmith and the stories of how the other characters came to live together. The mother's explanation of her actions is given the rhetorically powerful position at the end of the book, attesting that slavery is indeed the representative image of domination in the American cultural memory. But whereas Sethe and Paul D. try to come to terms with their shared past at Sweet Home and the haunting of their present life by the murdered child, the other characters in *A Mercy* either don't know about or don't fixate on Florens' struggle with her particular primal scene. They are each involved in trying to understand their own stories. The novel is held together by the parable of Florens' mistake—in Morrison's words "she was completely needy, yearning, selfless, 'my life is in you, I canted live without out you'… [the lesson is] do not give yourself over completely to anybody. At least you know she'll never do that again" (Rustin, n.p.). That theme unites the other stories, as each person attempts to recover some sense of self, to be less "needy, yearning, selfless." They each confront this problem in a different way, with common experiences scattered among them but no one history that all have in common, aside from their occupancy of Jacob's farm.

On the intrapersonal level, each character remembers a scene that formed their own "past" as a context for the present: Jacob revisits his experience at Jubilo, inspiring him to accrue property he had not previously dreamed of owning (including slaves, to which he is ethically and morally ambivalent); Rebecca recalls her horrific crossing of the Atlantic in the company of other female transportees; Lina recounts her indoctrination at the hands of the Presbyterians; Sorrow retells the loss of her firstborn child. On an interpersonal level, the novel itself stages a national primal scene that prompts its American readers to undergo the work of "rememory" vis-à-vis the colonial period. In going back to the pre-national past, Morrison articulates an alternative mytho-history, one that is not only about the invention of "a new white man" in the context of a signing Africanist presence. Rather, the colonial period as represented here is composed of many different individuals in a complex network of power relations negotiating a life together. This is not a teleological story of a nation formed for a single, unifying purpose (rebellion against European tyranny, political and religious). Nor does it make the creation of that nation, a hundred years after the events of the novel, into a historical inevitability. If anything, *A Mercy* remembers America as a place, a spatial proximity, where a great many different people came together, in a great many different ways, for many different purposes and to many different ends. While this does not depart from historical fact, it does displace a historiography that was much simpler because it was more uniformly white and male.

This alternative history of the community also has consequences for the individuals—all the novel's characters must create their own selves out of the crosshatching of their memories and their surroundings. Lina's story serves as the best example because she makes the strongest claim that unbroken continuity with the past is not a necessary condition for present action. Through the destruction of her village and her re-education by missionaries, Lina's "authentic" Native culture is lost beyond her ability to recall. But after the Presbyterians send Lina to Jacob, she develops a means to resist the ideologies which had been forced on her, even without having the "real" counter-ideology at hand:

> She decided to fortify herself by piecing together scraps of what her mother had taught her before dying in agony. Relying on memory and her own resources, she cobbled together neglected rites, merged Europe medicine with native, scripture with lore, and recalled or invented the hidden meaning of things. Found, in other words, a way to be in the world … Solitude would have crushed her had she not fallen into hermit skills and become one more thing that moved in the natural world. (48–9)

Lina performs this cobbling together a culture-of-one in temporal terms as piecing together the bits of the past. Morrison juxtaposes this resolution with the image of a chicken that nests in the corner of the kitchen—this blurring of the lines between the animal and human home speaks to Lina's revised identity as "one more thing that moved in the natural world." This is rememory performed on the levels of personal history, culture and, finally, ecology. Lina's cure for the solitude of being cut off from other people in the social world is to redefine her place in the natural world so that she is not cut off from other living things. By embracing the materials at hand, rather than longing for materials that are lost in the past or unavailable in the present, she finds a way to move, to save herself from being "crushed." Her galvanized identity is post-ethnic in the sense of no longer relying on an ascribed position in the world, but rather avowing, even on the limited basis on her own small life, her place from which to enunciate. After this realization, Lina becomes the reliable housekeeper of the farm, nursing the other women though sickness and childbirth.

Although Florens begins the novel and eventually writes her way out of the house, her escape is not the end of the book. The final section of the novel presents her mother's account of the day she asked Jacob to take her daughter away from Jubilo. Telling her she was taken into slavery, Florens' mother details the process by which she was ethnicized as "black" rather than human. When she arrived at Jubilo, Ortega had her raped and later raped her himself. It is to avoid this fate for her growing daughter that she begs Jacob to take Florens in payment, because "I saw the tall man see you as a human child, not pieces of eight" (166). This recognition of humanity—which we know from Jacob's version of the same event is informed by his own identity as an orphan—potentially undoes the dehumanizing process that tried ultimately to make her "pieces of eight." Yet we cannot forget that when Jacob accepts this bargain, he becomes a slave owner in a more sinister way than he has been up to this point. He does not, against all possibility, set Florens free. There is nothing so romantic or transcendent at work here—in the mother's words, "it was not a miracle. Bestowed by God. It was a mercy. Offered by a human" (166–67). Such may be the mercy we can expect in a world where no one stands outside the systems of political and social power. Systems of domination have been the historical norm, and Florens' mother closes the novel with an axiom for living with that reality: "[T]o be given dominion over another is a hard thing; to wrest dominion over another is a wrong thing; to give dominion of yourself to another is a wicked thing" (167). This suggests that while larger systems themselves are not quickly subject to reform, and revolutions may fail, something that persists in spite of those systems might mitigate the suffering they inflict. Lina pieces together a hybrid counter-culture, and Florens' mother chooses a less inhuman future for her daughter. These choices are by no means ideal, but they do break with the status quo, the situation at hand which has not been freely consented to.

A Mercy is, moreover, a novel of many unremarked lives, lives that were not marked down in the "pages of history" in the way that the biographies of the founding fathers were fashioned into a kind of hagiography. This unremarkable cast distinguishes it from a novel like Johnson's Dreamer, which attaches itself to a named "historical" personage. More importantly, the characters are revealed through making their own kinds of marks, most explicitly when Florens writes her story on the walls. The novel remembers a more complex community of individuals who lived in proximity with each other and in excess of conventional historiography's ability to account for their experiences. Thus, Morrison's novel complicates a normative vision of the land of the free. Although some who came there were visionaries and schemers, there was never a grand liberal design uniting everyone as "colonists," let alone "founding fathers." This early America is not even "America" in a national sense—there is no representation of unified, inevitable progression toward the Declaration of Independence, or any such "historical" event. There were, this novel remembers, only many different people interacting in many different ways, and the systems in place meant that most people suffered one way or another. Many such systems are still in place today. But also, and most importantly, there were acts of mercy. We can extend this to say that it is an ethos of human kindness, rather than faith in American goodness per se (its principles, its laws, its historical meaning), that the novel offers as a context for living in the present.

At the same time, the novel presents this moral vision by radically altering one of the prevailing stories by which America has tried to know itself. Readers who find it convincing and persuasive may have to rethink what it means to be Americans, in particular how they are united to other Americans by a past that is shared but not common to all. Lina tell Florens a mythic story featuring an eagle whose nest is disturbed by "a traveler" who arrives on the mountain top one day and, surveying the beautiful landscape, declares "'this is perfect, this is mine.'" His declaration causes a thunderous disruption and he attacks the eagle when she tries to protect her nest. The eagle is "still falling ... forever," and the eggs "hatch alone." When Florens asks if the chicks live, Lina answers, "we have." (62–3). Rather than being the inheritors of a national legacy, the novel suggests that Americans in the post-racial or post-cultural age are the orphaned children who are "still falling" through the contingencies of cause and effect, still haunted by the colonial proclamation. Rather than historical progress, the novel offers individual mercy as a way to ameliorate human suffering. In other words, the world will not become a better place because of the advent of a particular form of democracy. If it becomes a better place at all (and it may not) it will be through smaller, unremarkable, sometimes illegible actions.

This renewal of a sense of contingency, then, contradicts an established narrative of national destiny. In the future of *A Mercy*, it is not inevitable that America will be a shining beacon on a hill. If the past really did comprise many different kinds of people interacting in many various ways, then the future can emerge in several directions. Fragmentation within and between persons is the norm, not the aberration here. We tend to feel like the past is "fixed" because we know how it "really" turned out. We tend to think that the way things happened are the only way they could have happened. *A Mercy* reminds readers that things could have happened differently. What kind of ethics can we form if we believe ourselves and our communities to be other than part of a grand, hopefully benevolent design? Morrison's work figures a moral view where solidarity is not predicated on a unitary national identity, but rather the kindness that we may show to those with whom we live.

Works Cited

Anderson, Benedict. *Imaginary Communities*. NY: Verso, 1991
Hall, Stuart. "Ethnicity: Identity and Difference." *Radical America* 23 (1989): 9–20.
Mill, John Stuart. *Considerations on Representative Government*. NY: Harper & Brothers, 1862. Available from Project Gutenberg: http://www.gutenberg.org/ebooks/5669

Morrison, Toni. *Beloved*. Knopf. NY: Knopf, 1987.

—. *Playing in the Dark: Whiteness and the Literary Imagination*. Vintage. 1993.

—. *Paradise*. NY: Knopf, 1997.

—. *A Mercy*. NY: Knopf, 2008.

Rand, Naomi R. "Surviving What Haunts You: The Art of Invisibility in *Ceremony, The Ghost Writer*, and *Beloved*." *MELUS* 20 (3) (1995): 21–32.

Rhodes, Jewell Parker. "Toni Morrison's *Beloved*: Ironies of a 'Sweet Home' Utopia in a Dystopian Slave Society." *Utopian Studies* 1 (1) (1990): 77–92.

Rody, Caroline . *The Interethnic Imagination*. Oxford: Oxford University Press, 2009.

Rushdy, Ashraf H. A. "'Rememory': Primal Scenes and Constructions in Toni Morrison's Novels." *Contemporary Literature* 31 (3) (1990): 300–323.

Rustin, Susanna. "Predicting the Past." *The Guardian* October 31, 2008. http://www.guardian.co.uk/books/2008/nov/01/toni-morrison.

Sollors, Werner. *Beyond Ethnicity*. Oxford: Oxford University Press, 1986.

Steiner, Wendy. "The Clearest Eye." *New York Times Book Review* April 5, 1992. http://www.nytimes.com/1992/04/05/books/the-clearest-eye.html.

CONTRIBUTORS

Maria Rice Bellamy is an Assistant Professor of English at the College of Staten Island (CUNY), where she teaches courses in African-American, Multi-Ethnic American and Diasporic Literatures. Her critical essays have appeared in MELUS, *African-American Review*, and *The Explicator*. Her current book project, *Bridges to Memory: Post-memory in Contemporary Ethnic American Women's Fiction*, explores representations of inherited traumatic memory and the power of narrative to transform our understanding of self and trauma.

Sandra Cox is an Assistant Professor at Shawnee State University, where she teaches courses in Children's Literature, Young Adult Literature, and Multi-Ethnic American Literature. Her articles have appeared in *Antipodas, The Journal of Interdisciplinary Studies*, *Studies in American Indian Literature*, and *Southwestern American Literature*. She is currently at work on a book-length monograph which explores the ethical approaches to literary criticism of fiction by American writers of color.

Alice Eaton is an Associate Professor at Springfield College in Massachusetts, where she teaches courses in African-American and Post-colonial Literature. She serves as an office and newsletter editor for the Toni Morrison Society. Her writing has appeared in ARIEL and *the Chronicle of Higher Education*. Dr. Eaton has also contributed numerous entries to the multi-volume *African-American National Biography*, edited by Henry Louis Gates, II.

Gene Melton, II is a Senior Lecturer in English at North Carolina State University, where he teaches courses in British, American, and LGBTQ Literature, as well as first-year composition. His recent work focuses on race, masculinity, and sexuality in the fiction of Toni Morrison, the poetry of Essex Hemphill, and the memoirs of Richard Rodriguez, as well as on male homosexuality as a presence in British celebrity culture, in the United States military, and in online social networking communities.

Kathryn Mudgett, J. D., Ph. D., is an Associate Professor of Humanities at Massachusetts Maridame Academy, where she specializes in Nineteenth-Century American Law and Literature. She is the editor of *The Nautilus: A Maritime Journal of Literature and Culture.* Her book, *Writing the Seaman's Tale in Law and Literature: Dana, Melville, and Justice Story*, is forthcoming from AMS Press.

Terry Otten is Professor Emeritus of English and Kenneth Wray Professor in the Humanities at Wittenberg University. He is the author of four books, including *The Crime of Innocence in the Fiction of Toni Morrison.* His essays have appeared in more than twenty books and in various scholarly journals. Professor Otten was 1988 CASE and Carnegie Foundation Ohio Professor of the Year and National Bronze Medalist. He currently serves on the advisory board of The Arthur Miller Journal. Professor Otten now resides in Santa Fe, New Mexico.

Shirley A. (Holly) Stave is a Professor at the Louisiana Scholars' College at Northwestern State University, where she teaches seminars on the fiction of William Faulkner and Toni Morrison. She is the author of *The Decline of the Goddess: Women, Nature, and Culture in Thomas Hardy's Wessex*, the editor of *Gloria Naylor: Strategy and Technique, Magic and Myth,* and *Contested Intertextualities: Toni Morrison and the Bible.* Professor Stave is also a contributor to *The Cambridge Companion to Toni Morrison* and collection of essays in honor of Morrison's eightieth birthday celebration.

Charles Tedder is an Assistant Professor in the College of Individualized Studies at Metropolitan State University in Saint Paul, Minnesota, where he teaches courses in American Literature, Literary Theory, and Utopian Studies. His current scholarly projects include an edited collection on utopianism and diversity.